MAPPING THE SPATIAL DISTRIBUTION OF POVERTY USING SATELLITE IMAGERY IN THE PHILIPPINES

MARCH 2021

ADB

ASIAN DEVELOPMENT BANK

Contents

Tables, Figures, and Boxes

Boxes

Foreword

In the decades before the coronavirus disease (COVID-19) pandemic, the Philippine economy grew steadily. Real gross domestic product per capita, for instance, doubled from the late 1980s to 2019. The country's scorecard with respect to the Millennium Development Goals—particularly in promoting gender equality in primary, secondary, and tertiary education; advancing environmental sustainability by maintaining biological diversity; and decreasing debt service as a percentage of exports of goods and services—is also noteworthy.

Corresponding to economic growth, poverty in the Philippines declined during the same period. From 1985 to 2015, the proportion of people living below the extreme poverty line of $1.90 a day fell from 28% to 8%, an average reduction of 0.7 percentage points every year. While data in more recent years hint at faster poverty reduction in the country, other neighboring economies have shown faster pace of poverty reduction. Furthermore, the capacity of the Philippines to continue its improved trajectory of poverty reduction may be threatened by the COVID-19 pandemic.

Nevertheless, the Government of the Philippines remains committed to improving the lives of 110 million Filipinos. In fact, *AmBisyon Natin 2040*, the document that outlines the nation's vision and aspirations for the next 2 decades, articulates a country free of poverty, where all families will have a stable and high level of well-being. This vision also aligns with the first goal of the Agenda for Sustainable Development, which aims to eradicate extreme poverty by 2030.

As the Philippines accelerates its efforts to reduce poverty, the collection of accurate, timely, and granular data on poverty and socioeconomic disadvantage is critical. Currently, official poverty statistics are compiled by the Philippine Statistics Authority (PSA), using data collected through the triennial Family Income and Expenditure Survey. Generally, household income and expenditure surveys have sufficient sample sizes to generate reliable estimates at the national, state, and regional levels. The sample sizes, nevertheless, are insufficient to provide representative estimates at lower geographical levels, e.g., cities, municipalities, or villages. The estimates derived therefore may not be useful for formulating policies and designing poverty reduction programs for targeting the most disadvantaged groups in the country.

Designing surveys with large sample sizes, to yield reliable estimates at more disaggregated levels, is one potential solution, but it is often not feasible. Increasing survey sample sizes entails huge resources, which are often not available to national statistics offices (NSOs) and other organizations that implement surveys. To address this issue, some countries, including the Philippines, use the small area estimation methodology, whereby sample survey data are integrated with census and administrative data to produce more granular and reliable poverty statistics. This approach can, however, be constrained by the timeliness and currency of census and administrative data. Another alternative to achieve improved granularity and reliability is to employ innovative data sources of auxiliary data that are unlikely to have sampling errors.

In 2017, the Asian Development Bank (ADB) established the Data for Development knowledge management project, which seeks to enhance the capacities and capabilities of NSOs in the Asia and Pacific region. The project is designed to help NSOs face the challenge of generating volumes of data for evidence-based policymaking and for tracking the progress of development goals and targets. One of the project's components aims to generate more geographically disaggregated poverty statistics. This component follows research studies that employ satellite imagery, geospatial data, and powerful machine learning algorithms to augment conventional data collection and sample survey techniques. This methodology can be used to generate poverty estimates for more specific areas, with the results serving as inputs for policy formulation, program design, and targeted implementation of poverty reduction strategies.

Statisticians from ADB's Statistics and Data Innovation Unit within the Economic Research and Regional Cooperation Department collaborated with the PSA and the World Data Lab to conduct a feasibility study on poverty mapping using satellite imagery and relevant geospatial data. This country report documents the results of the feasibility study for the Philippines, which aimed to enhance the granularity, cost-effectiveness, and compilation of high-quality poverty statistics.

We hope the report will be useful for the PSA as well as NSOs across Asia and the Pacific, helping them consider innovative data sources as means of monitoring Sustainable Development Goal progress and delivering poverty-reduction programs.

Yasuyuki Sawada
Chief Economist and Director General
Economic Research and Regional Cooperation Department
Asian Development Bank

Acknowledgments

This country report on mapping poverty through data integration and artificial intelligence documents the results of a feasibility study conducted for the Philippines, which aimed to explore alternative data collection channels by combining traditional survey and estimation methods with innovative data sources.

The publication team was led by Arturo Martinez Jr, under the overall direction of Elaine Tan. Mildred Addawe and Arturo Martinez Jr wrote the report, with assistance from Joseph Albert Niño Bulan, Ron Lester Durante, Katharina Fenz, Martin Hoffer, Marymell Martillan, Thomas Mitterling, and Tomas Sako. Claire Dennis Mapa, Rosalinda Bautista, Minerva Eloisa Esquivias, Candido Astrologo Jr, Wilma Guillen, Severa de Costo, Bernadette Balamban, Patricia Anne San Buenaventura, Mechelle Viernes, Anna Jean Pascasio, Driesch Lucien Cortel, and Justine Angelo Bantang of the Philippine Statistics Authority, along with Asian Development Bank (ADB) consultants Katrina Miradora, Jan Arvin Lapuz, Zita Albacea, Jose Ramon Albert, Erniel Barrios, Joseph Ryan Lansangan, and Bastian Zaini, all contributed to works that were used as inputs and references for the report. WDL's Kristofer Hamel and ADB's Rana Hasan and Kaushal Joshi provided insightful feedback that helped refine the findings of the study, while participants at the Big Data Analytics workshop and colleagues from the Philippine Statistical Research and Training Institute contributed valuable comments and feedback.

Celia Reyes and the Community-Based Monitoring System Network Office Team provided the Community Based Monitoring System poverty data used in the validation of this study's machine learning-based poverty predictions. Francois Fonteneau of the Partnership in Statistics for Development in the 21st Century, Arman Bidarbakht-Nia and Sharita Serrao of the United Nations Economic and Social Commission for Asia and the Pacific, Haoyi Chen and Yongyi Min of the United Nations Statistics Division, Roy Van der Weide of the World Bank, and Daniel Clarke and Jonggun Lee of the Organisation for Economic Co-operation and Development provided valuable insights during the conceptualization of the technical assistance project. Criselda De Dios and Iva Sebastian, with the assistance of Ma. Roselia Babalo, Oth Marulou Gagni, Aileen Gatson, and Rose Anne Dumayas, provided operational support throughout the project.

The cover of this report was designed by Ron Lester Durante. Manuscript editing was performed by Paul Dent, while the publication's layout, page design, and typesetting were provided by Principe Nicdao.

Abbreviations

ADB	Asian Development Bank
ARMM	Autonomous Region of Muslim Mindanao
CBMS	Community-Based Monitoring System
CNN	convolutional neural network
FIES	Family Income and Expenditure Survey
GEO	geostationary
GMM	Gaussian mixture model
km	kilometer
km^2	square kilometer
LEO	low Earth orbit
m	meter
MDG	Millennium Development Goal
MEO	medium Earth orbit
NCR	National Capital Region
NSO	national statistics office
OLS	ordinary least squares
PSA	Philippine Statistics Authority
PSS	Philippine Statistical System
RGB	red, green, blue
RMSE	root mean square error
SAE	small area estimation
SDG	Sustainable Development Goal
VIIRS	Visible Infrared Imaging Radiometer Suite

1 Background

1.1 Introduction

The Millennium Development Goals (MDGs), active from 2000 to 2015, achieved significant milestones in addressing global poverty in its different dimensions—education, health, gender equality, and related areas. The MDG target was to halve the 1990 poverty rate by 2015. By the end of 2015, the proportion of world population living on less than $1.90 declined to 10.1%.[1] The primary school net enrollment rate increased from 83% in 2000 to 91% in 2015. Gender disparity in primary, secondary, and tertiary education was reduced in developing regions, with more girls studying in school and at university over the 15-year period. In health, the under-5 mortality rate and the maternal mortality ratio also dropped significantly worldwide. In the economies of Asia and the Pacific, the MDG poverty target was far exceeded: the proportion of people living on less than $1.25 a day fell from 53% in 1990 to 14% in 2012 (MDG Monitor 2016). More specifically, income poverty in the Philippines, based on official poverty lines, decreased from 34.4% in 1991 to 16.7% in 2018.[2]

The data compiled for MDG monitoring provided a broad picture of socioeconomic progress attained by a country relative to other national economies. However, such data were inadequate to show how different segments of a country's population fared, and which of these segments succeeded or lagged in terms of achieving the MDG targets (ADB 2017). This is deemed problematic from the perspective of policy formulation and program design for those marginalized segments of the population.

The inequality of outcomes achieved under the MDGs paved the way for the "leave no one behind" principle of the 2030 Agenda for Sustainable Development. This principle requires appropriate Sustainable Development Goal (SDG) indicators to be estimated for different segments of a country's population, i.e., based on income class, gender, ethnicity, geographic location, and other relevant dimensions. This requires more granular data on population groups, extending the focus beyond national trends and averages, and toward identifying those segments of the population that are being left out with respect to specific development targets (ADB 2017).

The Philippine Statistics Authority (PSA) is committed to supporting the data requirements to accurately monitor the country's progress in achieving the SDGs.[3] The PSA has carried out several initiatives to address the need for granular poverty estimates that can meet disaggregated data requirements. In 2005, the PSA (then the National Statistical Coordination Board)[4] started generating small area estimates of poverty within all cities and municipalities in the country,[5] through a project funded by the World Bank. In the same year, the agency also

---

[1] During the MDG implementation period, the extreme poverty line used was $1.25 a day, in 2008 purchasing power parities (PPP).

[2] The 1991 and 2018 official poverty lines are based on different sets of CPI market basket.

[3] Through PSA Resolution No. 4 Series of 2016, Enjoining Government Agencies to Provide Data Support to the Sustainable Development Goals (SDGs), the PSA Board directs all government agencies to provide the data requirements for monitoring the SDGs based on an indicator framework prepared by the National Economic and Development Authority, the PSA, and other government institutions.

[4] The Philippine Statistical Act of 2013 created the PSA, which consolidated the major statistical agencies engaged in primary data collection and compilation of secondary data, i.e., the National Statistics Office, the National Statistical Coordination Board, the Bureau of Agricultural Statistics, and the Bureau of Labor and Employment Statistics.

[5] Since the initial release, small area estimates of poverty have been produced triennially through several projects funded by the World Bank, the Government of Australia, and the Government of the Philippines. The estimates are available for reference years 2000, 2003, 2006, 2009, 2012, and 2015. Despite these regular releases, the small area poverty estimates have yet to be adopted by the Philippine Statistical System as part of the official statistics, although this statistical activity is included in the Philippine Statistical Development Program.

produced poverty estimates for eight of the 14 basic sectors[6] of Philippine society considered "disadvantaged" under the Philippine Social Reform and Poverty Alleviation Act. In 2018, the PSA increased nearly fourfold the sample size of the triennial Family Income and Expenditure Survey (FIES), i.e., from 50,000 households to 180,000 households, to provide reliable poverty estimates for all provinces and highly urbanized cities.

The move toward subnational estimates of poverty helps build a more accurate profile of the poor. From 2006 to 2015, chronic poverty[7] was prevalent in the Philippine provinces of Lanao del Sur, Maguindanao, Northern Samar, Sarangani, and Zamboanga del Norte, which are consistently classified as the country's poorest cluster of provinces.[8] At a more disaggregated geographic level, of the nine municipalities with poverty rates higher than 70% in 2015, seven were situated in Lanao del Sur, one in Misamis Occidental and one in Northern Samar. Looking at the sectoral level, the disadvantaged segments of the population with the most persistently high poverty rates were farmers, fishers, and children.

For poverty reduction programs to be effective in identifying which segments of the population need priority solutions, it is imperative to sustain, as well as continuously improve, the generation of poverty estimates at the subnational level. However, the compilation of granular estimates of poverty, particularly generation of small area estimates, is impeded by several constraints: (i) the technical and computational expertise involved in small area estimation (SAE); (ii) methodological issues, such as variation in reference years when census and survey data are merged; and (iii), timeliness in generating the estimates.

The use of innovative data sources has the potential to address the limitations and, at the same time, enhance poverty estimates generated from conventional data sources. For instance, data from satellites and mobile phones may be used in small area poverty estimation techniques to measure economic well-being. In Uganda, there is an ongoing initiative to measure granular estimates of poverty through roof-counting conducted using satellite imagery (UN Global Pulse 2018). Similarly, in Malawi, Nigeria, Rwanda, and Tanzania, satellite imagery and machine learning have been combined to predict fine-grained poverty estimates (Jean et al. 2016). As opposed to traditional data sources (such as censuses, surveys, and administrative data), these new and technological sources can produce more granular data that can be processed immediately after collection (Castelan et al. 2019).

To provide more relevant and accurate data for policy design and targeted initiatives, the Asian Development Bank (ADB), through its Data for Development technical assistance project, conducted country case studies on applying innovative data analytics to provide disaggregation for select SDG indicators. This report presents a detailed discussion of the alternative methodologies for generating more geographically disaggregated estimates of poverty and population for the monitoring of SDG indicators.

1.2   Sustainable Development Goal Data of the Philippines

The Philippine Development Plan, the medium-term directions of the Government of the Philippines, not only lays out the socioeconomic agenda of the government for 2017 to 2022, but also provides an overview of the country's commitment to the 2030 Agenda for Sustainable Development (NEDA 2017). The SDGs are integrated into the government's targets for quality education, decent work, reduced inequality, climate action, peace, justice, strong institutions, and effective partnerships (UN DESA 2019).

---

[6] Poverty estimates for farmers, fishers, children, women, youth, migrant and formal sector workers, senior citizens, and individuals residing in urban areas are available for reference years 2000, 2003, 2006, 2009, 2012, 2015, and 2018. Likewise, poverty estimates for self-employed and unpaid family workers, which serve as proxy data for workers in the informal sector, are available for 2006, 2009, 2012, 2015, and 2018. Furthermore, estimates for poor population residing in rural areas are available for 2015 and 2018 and poverty incidence among persons aged 15 years and over with disability are available for 2018 (PSA 2020).

[7] Chronic poverty is defined in this report as the situation where poverty persists in an area for an extended period, i.e., provinces are consistently grouped in the poorest cluster for more than 5 years.

[8] In the Philippines' Official Poverty Statistics, provinces are grouped into five clusters, where Cluster 1 refers to the bottom or poorest cluster of provinces and Cluster 5 refers to the least poor cluster of provinces.

In the Philippines, the PSA is the main data custodian for SDG monitoring, based on PSA Resolution No.4 Series of 2016, Enjoining Government Agencies to Provide Data Support to the SDGs. An assessment of the 244 SDG indicators[9] shows that, in the Philippines, 102 were classified as Tier 1 indicators, 55 were Tier 2 indicators, 74 were Tier 3 indicators, and the remaining 13 (5.3%) were deemed not relevant to the country. Based on the PSA's consultation workshops with various stakeholders, of the 102 Tier 1 indicators, data for about 32% were available from PSA censuses, surveys, and administrative sources; 67% were available from the surveys and administrative sources of other government organizations; and 1% were available from international data sources. The status of available disaggregated data is provided in Figure 1.1. The PSA disseminates the SDG data through SDG Watch, a web-based compilation of the SDG indicators for specific targets, along with baseline and current data and the source of data for each indicator.

Figure 1.1: Number of Available Disaggregated Data per Sustainable Development Goal

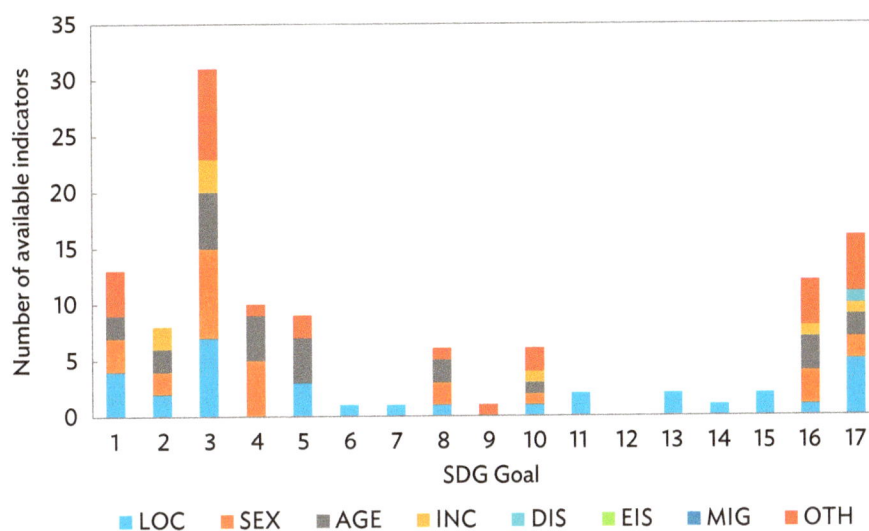

LOC = location or spatial disaggregation, INC = income quintiles/deciles, DIS = disability, EIS = ethnicity and indigenous status, MIG = migration status, OTH = others.
Source: Philippine Statistics Authority. Graphics generated by the study team.

Population and poverty indicators are among the most-cited development indicators. These indicators serve as critical inputs in the design, formulation, implementation, monitoring, and evaluation of sociodemographic policies and programs. Although most of the SDG indicators concerning poverty are classified as Tier 1 in the Philippines, there is room for improvement. For instance, there is an issue of granularity when generating official poverty data from the FIES. This survey has samples sizes that are large enough to provide nationally and regionally representative estimates, along with estimates that fall within acceptable levels of reliability when further disaggregating by provinces and/or highly urbanized cities. However, FIES sample sizes are not large enough to provide reliable estimates at more granular levels, such as municipalities and barangays (villages), and such estimates are crucial for more effective programs to target poverty.

The PSA compiles official poverty statistics that are available at the national, regional, provincial, and highly urbanized city levels. Small area estimates of poverty, which are generated on a project basis, are available at the

---

9   The PSA conducted the assessment in 2016, when the number of approved global SDG indicators was 244. As of March 2020, there were 247 global SDG indicators, but 12 of these were indicators repeated across different targets, so that the total number of unique indicators was only 231. https://unstats.un.org/sdgs/indicators/indicators-list/.

municipality and city levels. Meanwhile, the Community Based Monitoring System[10]—used in the preparation of local development plans, including budgeting at the local level—generates and releases monetary and nonmonetary poverty estimates for selected provinces, municipalities, cities, and barangays in the Philippines. The system also serves as an SDG localization instrument (Reyes et al. 2019).

The PSA generates population data from the national census, and these are available at the national, regional, provincial, city, and municipality levels. Meanwhile, population projections are released at only the national, regional, and provincial levels.

1.3   ADB Technical Assistance

ADB's Data for Development project aims to support the statistical capacity of national statistics offices (NSOs) in Asia and the Pacific, helping them comply with the many and varied data requirements for policymaking and monitoring of development goals and targets. The project has three major components: (i) subnational disaggregation of data to monitor the SDGs, (ii) enhanced compilation of national accounts and other key economic indicators, and (iii) provision of strategic inputs for the modernization of national statistical systems to inform policy design and statistical capacity-building initiatives of the global statistical system (ADB 2017).

The first component focuses on strengthening the capacity of NSOs to generate fine-grained data for policies and programs targeted to vulnerable sectors of society. Outputs of the component include a technical manual on disaggregation of official statistics, knowledge-sharing workshops, and case studies on various applications of innovative data disaggregation for select SDG indicators (ADB 2017). The technical manual includes an inventory of various SAE methodologies; techniques on using innovative data sources (such as satellite images, mobile phone records, or social media datasets) to yield granular data for official statistics; and relevant issues in using such data. The project also supports a series of strategically designed training programs, which aim to strengthen the skills of participating NSO staff in applying statistical methods that can be used to meet the disaggregated data requirements of the SDGs. Finally, the project includes two country case studies on the specific application of SAE and innovative data analytics to the disaggregation of poverty data.

The Data for Development project is connected to the Cape Town Global Action Plan for Sustainable Development Data and ADB's Strategy 2030 framework. The goal of the action plan is to provide capacity building on SDG indicators to developing and least-developed countries and to strengthen national statistical systems in meeting the statistical needs of the 2030 Agenda for Sustainable Development (UN DESA 2017). Meanwhile, ADB's Strategy 2030 sets development goals for Asia and the Pacific, including those linked to major global commitments, the SDGs, and related financing of the Agenda for Sustainable Development. ADB plans to expand its scope to eliminate extreme poverty across the Asia and Pacific region, and extend initiatives in education, health, and social protection (ADB 2018).

In line with the statistical capacity-building activities under the first component of the Data for Development project, NSO staff in participating ADB member countries are first introduced to the basic concepts and techniques of SAE; basic R programming; and application of big data sources (particularly geospatial data) on the compilation and disaggregation of data for select socioeconomic indicators within the SDGs, including poverty-related statistics. These staff are then trained in machine learning algorithms using satellite imagery and geospatial data, particularly random forest estimation for population mapping; convolutional neural networks (CNNs), a type of deep-learning algorithm; and ridge regression for poverty mapping. Data for Development promotes the use of open platforms and nonproprietary data to sustain the ongoing generation of estimates. Hence, most of the tools

---

[10] As of February 2019, CBMS was undertaken in 78 provinces (33 of which are conducting the system province-wide), 1,091 municipalities, and 111 cities, with a total of 30,827 barangays. In April 2019, the CBMS law "An Act Establishing the Community Based Monitoring System" was passed where the Philippine Statistics Authority (PSA) was designated as the lead implementing agency of CBMS.

used during the training workshops are nonproprietary and can be accessed for free. This allows greater scope for scaling up and institutionalization of alternative data source techniques within individual NSOs.

In September 2020, ADB published *A Special Supplement to Key Indicators for Asia and the Pacific 2020*, which provided the initial findings on poverty mapping using artificial intelligence. Hence, some of the discussions presented in the Key Indicators Supplement are reproduced here, albeit, more specific details on this technique relevant to the case study conducted in the Philippines are presented in this report.

1.4   Overview of the Methodology

This study implemented the methodology used in the Stanford research on combining satellite imagery and machine learning to predict poverty (Jean et al. 2016). This requires training a machine learning algorithm, i.e., a CNN, to identify and classify image features.

Using daytime satellite images as input, the CNN predicts the intensity of night lights, which is a valid proxy for data on economic activity or economic development. These satellite images are available at more disaggregated levels than traditional data sources. While going through the learning stage of predicting night light intensity, the CNN begins to recognize image patterns associated with light intensity, which can serve as inputs in the prediction of

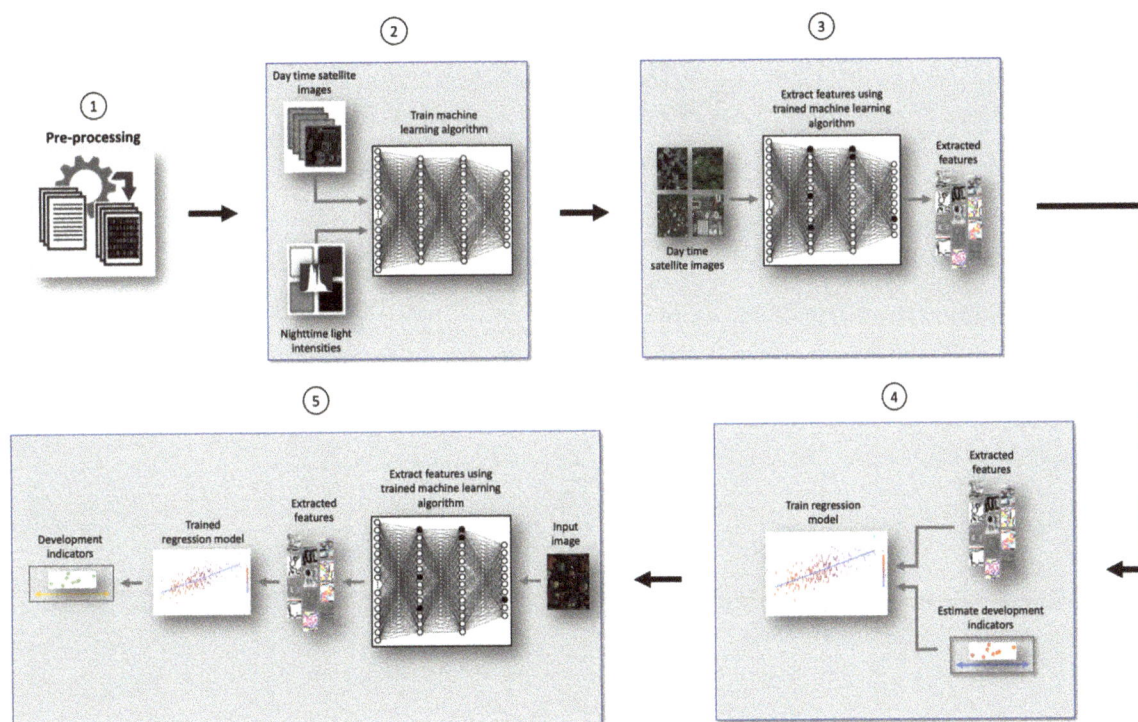

Figure 1.2: Methodological Design for Predicting Poverty Using Satellite Imagery

Notes: The data requirements are granular poverty data, daytime satellite images, and nighttime light intensities. Step 1 cleans and preprocesses the data. Step 2 pretrains a machine learning algorithm to categorize daytime images into various intensity levels of night light. Step 3 draws the visual features of the last layer of the trained machine learning algorithm. Step 4 finds the average image features to make the space enclosed in grids consistent with the level of available development-labelled images. Regression is done to explain the relationship between the image features and the government-compiled poverty estimates. Step 5 summarizes Steps 2 to 4, from extracting images to predicting poverty.
Source: Graphics generated by the study team.

poverty estimates. The more specific image-based information can then be aggregated to a level consistent with government-compiled poverty estimates. Using a transfer-learning technique, where a pretrained network on the ImageNet database sets a label to a large database of images, can accelerate the training process and minimize the volume of data needed for training.

The second step concentrates on the use of a trained CNN as a function that compresses the multidimensional input of image data into a single vector. This vector has hundreds of features, with corresponding values for each feature. These features illustrate what the network identifies within the image: they have advantages over the raw pixel values, especially because the convolutional layers scan over the image using kernels, so that it does not matter where the features appear within the image.

The third step entails deriving the average value of each feature for the referenced geographic areas, enabling the merging of the grid-based image features with the government-compiled poverty data.

In the fourth and final training step, ridge regression is applied to examine the relationship between the image features as predicting variables and the government-compiled poverty data.[11] The trained CNN and ridge parameters are then employed to predict poverty using solely a daytime image.

1.5   Socioeconomic Background of the Philippines

General Information

The Philippines is an archipelagic country in Southeast Asia. It is surrounded by the Sulu Sea to the southwest, the Celebes Sea to the south, the Pacific Ocean to the east, and the Philippine Sea to the north and west (Brittanica 2019). The country has a territory of more than 300,000 square kilometers (km^2) covered by a total of 7,641 islands (Government of the Philippines 2019). The Philippines is geographically disaggregated into three major island groups, i.e., Luzon, Visayas, and Mindanao, with 17 regions, 81 provinces, 146 cities, and 1,488 municipalities.

In 2019, the Philippines had a population of 108.3 million, with an annual population growth rate of 1.6% from 2014 to 2019 (ADB 2020). The country had a population density of 337 people per km^2 in 2015 (PSA 2016). More than half (51.2%) of the Philippine population lived in urban areas in 2015 (PSA 2019). Based on the 2019 Asian Development Outlook, Metro Manila, the country's national capital region, is the most congested city in Asia (ADB 2019). It is also the most densely populated region in the country, with a population of 12.9 million and a population density of 20,785 people per km^2 in 2015 (PSA 2016). The next most-congested provinces are those adjacent to Metro Manila: Rizal, Cavite, Laguna, Bulacan, and Pampanga (Figure 1.3).

Economic and Social Well-Being

The Philippines is one of the emerging economies of Southeast Asia, with its gross domestic product expanding by an average of 6.4% a year from 2010 to 2017 (ADB 2018). However, in comparison to other Association of Southeast Asian Nations member states, the Philippines lags behind Singapore, Brunei Darussalam, Malaysia, Thailand, and Indonesia with respect to gross domestic product per capita (Figure 1.4).

Since the early 2000s, the Government of the Philippines has worked toward achieving inclusive growth, as demonstrated by decreasing poverty rates and improved income inequality (World Bank 2019). From 2006 to 2018, the country's poverty rate, based on the nationally defined poverty line, decreased from 29.1% to 16.7%,[12]

---

[11] Hofer et al. (2020) also used random forest estimation as an alternative to ridge regression and found similar results.
[12] The 2006 and 2018 poverty lines are based on different sets of CPI market basket.

Figure 1.3: Population Density by Province and Highly Urbanized City, 2015

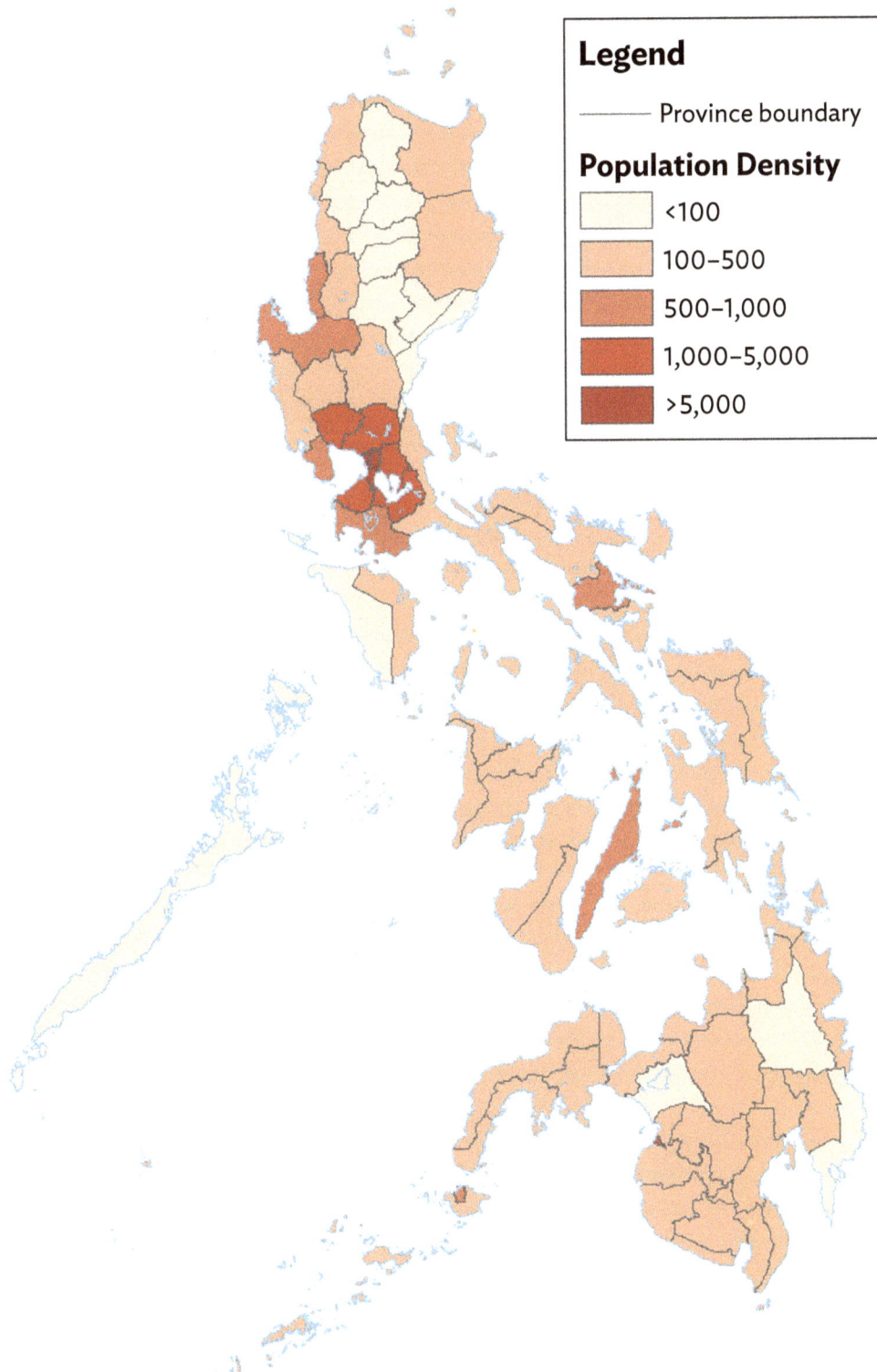

Legend

—— Province boundary

Population Density

- <100
- 100–500
- 500–1,000
- 1,000–5,000
- >5,000

Source: Philippine Population Density (Based on the 2015 Census of Population). Philippine Statistics Authority.

while the Gini coefficient (a measure of income inequality) decreased from 45.8% to 42.7%. These improvements are explained not just by continued economic growth, but also by reforms and investments that have created employment and delivered better social protection (NEDA 2019).

While unemployment in the Philippines has declined significantly, underemployment remains high. Although many Filipino workers have shifted from agriculture to the service sector, a large proportion of these workers are engaged in jobs on the minimum income (World Bank 2019).

Figure 1.4: Gross Domestic Product per Capita of Association of Southeast Asian Nations Member States ($)

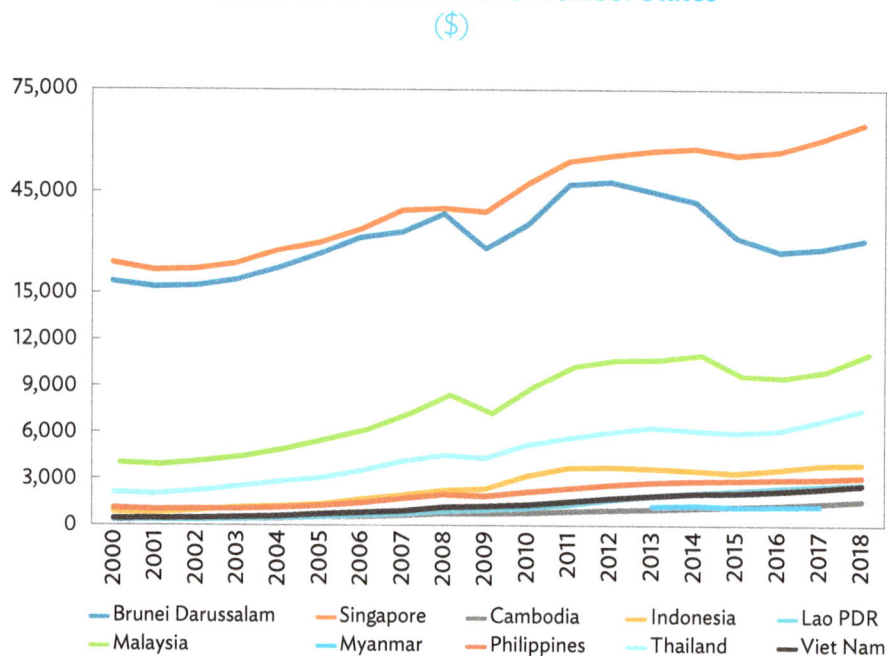

Lao PDR = Lao People's Democratic Republic.
Note: Myanmar gross domestic product data not available for 2000 to 2012 and for 2018.
Source: Asian Development Bank Key Indicators Database 2019.

Poverty Reduction Programs in the Philippines

While the national poverty rate declined by 12.4 percentage points from 2006 to 2018, significant pockets of poverty persist throughout the Philippines, particularly in the south of the country, where the Autonomous Region of Muslim Mindanao and Caraga remain the poorest regions. The latest estimates also indicate that in several municipalities—Kapai, Marogong, Lumbaca-Unayan, and Piagapo in Lanao del Sur Province; Concepcion in Misamis Occidental Province; and Nunungan and Tangcal in Lanao del Norte Province—more than 60% of the population are living below the poverty line. Through a number of well-funded initiatives, the Government of the Philippines has recognized the need for continuous efforts to further reduce and eventually eliminate poverty in these areas.

One of these initiatives is the sustained implementation of the Conditional Cash Transfer Program,[13] which was launched in 2008 to augment the incomes of poor families by providing cash transfers with conditions on child education and health as well as maternal health. In addition, the government is implementing the Social Pension Program, which provides monthly stipends to impoverished senior citizens to supplement their daily sustenance and other medical necessities, along with the Unconditional Cash Transfer Program, which offers cash allowances to poor households and individuals who are not covered by reduced income tax rates and are affected by price inflation. The government is also continuously rolling out the *Kapit-Bisig Laban sa Kahirapan*–Comprehensive and Integrated Delivery of Social Services (Kalahi-CIDSS). This poverty alleviation program, which started in 2003, aims to empower small communities in targeted municipalities by enhancing delivery of basic services, reducing poverty, and improving local governance (DSWD 2018, 2019).

Considering the multidimensional aspects of poverty, the government has implemented a number of targeted programs. The National Health Insurance Program provides inexpensive and readily available health-care services for all Filipinos, as well as comprehensive health benefits for indigent families. The Supplemental Feeding Program aims to improve the nutrition of disadvantaged school-aged children. The Training for Work Scholarship Program, the Expanded Students' Grants-In-Aid Program for Poverty Alleviation, the Commission on Higher Education Scholarship Program for 4Ps beneficiaries, and the Scholarship Benefits and Student Financial Assistance Program all help to ensure continuous education and skills training of children from impoverished households.

Policy Uses of Geographically Disaggregated Poverty Estimates

Information identifying the specific needs of the most impoverished segments of the population is needed for poverty alleviation programs to have greater effectiveness. The production of granular data on poverty is therefore necessary for more efficient targeting and implementation of such programs.

As early as 2003, the PSA published official poverty statistics at the provincial level for reference years 1997 and 2000. However, there was a continuous call for disaggregated poverty estimates referencing a greater number of years. In 2005, the PSA, in collaboration with the World Bank, undertook the poverty mapping project, which resulted in the generation and release of (unofficial) municipality-level poverty estimates based on SAE techniques.

Since the inaugural release of these estimates in 2005, various national and local government units, as well as private and international organizations, have capitalized on small area estimates of poverty in formulating and implementing scores of socioeconomic policies and programs on poverty reduction. The Philippines' Department of Social Welfare and Development used the estimates as reference in identifying poor municipalities for (i) the National Household Targeting System for Poverty Reduction data collection; (ii) the Kalahi-CIDSS Program; (iii) assistance for families affected by typhoon Yolanda (Haiyan) in Western Visayas; (iv) the Student Grants-In-Aid Program for Poverty Alleviation in the Cordillera Administrative Region; and (v) the Cash-For-Training Program in the SOCCSKSARGEN Region. Many local government units—Negros Occidental; Pangasinan; the municipality of Nabas in Aklan; the city of Baguio; and the municipalities of Itogon, La Trinidad, Sablan, and Tuba in Benguet—also referred to the small area estimates as inputs in developing localized socioeconomic profiles and to identify areas requiring poverty reduction initiatives. The provincial governments of Aklan, La Union, Negros Occidental, Pangasinan, and Southern Leyte used the estimates in assessing the implementation of their poverty

---

[13] The result of the first and second impact evaluation studies on the CCT Program in the Philippines conducted in 2011 and 2013, respectively, indicates improvement in health service utilization and school enrollment. More specifically, the studies show increase in access to antenatal care and postnatal care; decrease in cases of severe stunting; improvement in enrollment among children 3 to 15 years old and school attendance among 3–17 years old (ADB 2020). In addition, the third impact evaluation study undertaken in 2017 to 2019 reveals that the program also promotes awareness and utilization of modern family planning methods; contributes to household welfare; decreases the proportion of working children among recipients; and influences the determination of children to succeed in school despite hardships (PIDS 2020).

reduction programs. Meanwhile, ADB, Agencia Española de Cooperación Internacional para el Desarrollo, the Early Childhood Care and Development Council, the German Technical Cooperation, the Philippine National Red Cross, Plan Philippines, the United Nations Children's Fund (UNICEF), the United Nations Population Fund, and the World Bank have all employed small area estimates in various poverty-related alleviation programs in different areas of the Philippines (PSA 2013, 2016).

Use of Innovative Data Sources in Generating Philippine Development Statistics

Conventional data sources—particularly censuses, surveys, vital registrations, and administrative reporting systems—are important in gathering information on various topics at aggregated and disaggregated levels. However, there are corresponding financial, technical, and operational challenges in generating information from these data collection vehicles. Some countries do not regularly conduct censuses and surveys due to budget constraints. In addition, there can be issues with the timeliness of data being released via conventional sources. Innovative data sources, on the other hand, are deemed more cost-effective, have wider coverage, and can generate more granular data (often in real-time). The PSA acknowledges the merits of innovative data sources in complementing conventional sources to yield high quality, timely, and disaggregated data. In this context, the authority has embarked on several undertakings and partnerships with local and international institutions to explore new data sources. In 2016, the PSA established the Task Force on Big Data for Official Statistics, to spearhead the "formulation of rules, standards, and protocols, facilitate engagements with stakeholders involved, set up statistical quality standards and validation mechanism for Big Data for use in official statistics" (PSA 2016). The task force is comprised of representatives and resource staff from the public and private sectors, academia, and international organizations. Also in 2016, the PSA, together with the Partnership in Statistics for Development in the 21st Century (PARIS21), held the Country Workshop on Access to New Data Sources for Official Statistics (PSA 2016). The aim of the workshop was to assess the possibility of capturing data from nonconventional sources within the public and private sectors—telecommunications companies, government regulatory agencies, market research companies, data analytics companies, and other related organizations—to address the data requirements of the SDG indicators in the Philippines.

The PSA, in collaboration with the Department of Information and Communications Technology and the International Telecommunication Union, is conducting the pilot project Big Data for Measuring the Information Society. The objectives of this project are to (i) demonstrate how big data can be used for information and communication technology (ICT) measurement; (ii) show how big data can be used to produce new ICT indicators, complement existing ICT indicators, and fill data gaps on core indicators and ICT-related indicators within the SDG framework; and (iii) enhance data collection, benchmarks, and methodologies to measure the information society through improved disaggregation of data for specific indicators.

The latest version of the Philippine Statistical Development Program[14] for 2018–2023 stipulates the "strengthening of the data ecosystem to include the exploration of use of big data and citizen-generated data as possible sources of official statistics" as one of its goals. The case study covered by this report is therefore consistent with the efforts of the PSA in capitalizing on new types of data sources (PSA 2018).

---

14 The Philippine Statistical Development Program is the Philippines' local counterpart of the National Strategies for the Development of Statistics. It is an inventory of the Philippine Statistical System's medium-term directions, thrusts, and priorities for the production and dissemination of statistical information for the government, the private sector, and the general public.

2 How Are Poverty Statistics Estimated?

2.1 Conventional Estimation of Poverty Statistics

When used for poverty estimation, data can highlight the plight of the poorest and most marginalized in society. Data can help specify their living conditions and make them visible in socioeconomic programs. This requires compiling poverty profiles that include accurate identities of the poor, the depth of their poverty, locations of impoverished communities, and reasons why people are poor. Access to more disaggregated and granular poverty statistics can respond to some of these requirements and provide a better view of the characteristics of the poor. Analysis of the poverty profile can be conducted with confidence if the poverty data are available at disaggregated levels.

In the Philippines, official poverty statistics are generated at the national, regional, and provincial levels, as well as for highly urbanized cities. Similarly, official poverty data in most developing nations of Asia and the Pacific are compiled at the national, regional, provincial, or other less granular levels. NSOs and development partners in most of these countries, including the Philippines, acknowledge the need for more geographically disaggregated poverty data to ensure outcome-focused policymaking and best use of development resources.

Fine-grained poverty data can serve as inputs for a range of poverty reduction policies and programs, including cash transfer programs and employment facilitation. These data can also be used for monitoring and evaluating ongoing poverty reduction initiatives, with poverty data patterns and trends showing the impacts that measures such as tax reforms and cash-for-work programs might be having on the poor.

Considering the significance of poverty data in formulating policies and evaluating programs, statisticians go to great lengths to generate poverty numbers that are both accurate and objective. To objectively measure poverty, the first step is to identify the appropriate welfare indicator for classifying a household or individual as poor or nonpoor. Income and expenditure are the widely used welfare indicators. However, there are corresponding strengths and weaknesses in using one metric over the other. The Philippines uses income rather than expenditure as the welfare metric for identifying a family or individual as poor or nonpoor.[15] When responding to the Family Income and Expenditure Survey (FIES), one of the major data sources of official poverty estimates in the Philippines, information about income is deemed easier to recall and report than are details of expenditure (PSA 2003).

Once the welfare indicator is selected, the next step in objectively measuring poverty is to determine the poverty line. Many countries, including the Philippines, use the "cost of basic needs" method in measuring absolute poverty. Absolute poverty is characterized by extreme scarcity of basic needs such as food, safe drinking water, sanitary facilities, health, shelter, education, and information (UN 1995). Poverty lines in the Philippines refer to the minimum income required to meet basic food and nonfood needs such as clothing, fuel, light and water, adequate housing, transportation and communication, health and education, nondurable furnishing, household operations, and personal care and effects. The World Bank, which provides intercountry comparisons of poverty, has also established an absolute poverty line of $1.90 a day at 2011 purchasing power parity. Meanwhile, more economically advanced countries construct relative poverty lines. The relative poverty line normally considers the median income level needed to satisfy the country's average living standard as a point of comparison with the incomes of families or individuals who might be poor (UN 2005).

---

[15] The "poor" is officially defined as those families or individuals whose incomes fall below the poverty line set by the National Economic and Development Authority, and/or those who cannot afford in a sustained manner to provide their minimum basic needs of food, health, education, housing, and other essential amenities of life (PSA 2017).

The "cost of basic needs" approach determines a food basket that satisfies the minimum nutritional requirements of the World Health Organization and the Food and Agriculture Organization of the United Nations. Different countries have different minimum nutritional standards, depending on the population's age-sex structure, average weights, and activity levels. The Philippines has established a set of food bundles that fulfill the minimum requirement of 2,000 calories per person per day, regardless of age, sex, and place of residence (PSA 2007).

In the Philippines, the generation of official poverty data starts with the calculation of the food poverty line and the general poverty line. The food poverty line is estimated by costing the provincial food bundle using actual prices for agricultural and nonagricultural food items. To derive the general poverty line, the food poverty line is divided by the ratio of actual food expenditures to total basic expenditure, to account for the cost of basic nonfood needs. The general poverty line is then compared with the income data collected from the FIES to estimate poverty rates and other measures of poverty in the Philippines (PSA 2017).

Applying the equivalence scale is another approach to poverty estimation. The approach presumes that families or households having similar income or expenditure levels do not necessarily share the same level of well-being. A household's well-being depends on its composition or size, e.g., number of employed adults, infants, children, and ageing members. The equivalence scale approach calculates the household's per capita income or expenditure by dividing the total income or expenditure by the household size, then comparing the per capita estimate with the poverty line. Aside from household size and composition, poverty estimates can also be adjusted to account for household members' age by setting weights for different age ranges.

Household income and expenditure surveys and living standards surveys are the most common household data collection tools in poverty measurement. In the Philippines, the FIES is one of the major data sources of official poverty estimates. Like other household surveys, income and expenditure surveys, living standards surveys, and the FIES generally have sample sizes that are not large enough to provide reliable poverty data at sufficiently disaggregated levels. While NSOs acknowledge the merits of producing more disaggregated estimates for policymaking, they are also constrained by limited financial resources. Censuses and administrative-based data are alternative sources of more granular estimates, but there are also cost factors and benefits associated with these.

Given the limitations of household surveys, statisticians employ SAE techniques to generate more disaggregated poverty data. These methods combine survey data with auxiliary information from other data sources, such as census or administrative sources, to produce more granular poverty estimates. The World Bank, for instance, developed a poverty mapping methodology using SAE, which was implemented in at least 70 countries, including the Philippines and other developing nations across Asia and the Pacific. In the Philippines, the SAE initiative started through the Poverty Mapping Project implemented by the PSA (then National Statistical Coordination Board), with technical and funding assistance from the World Bank.

The project's main outputs were small area estimates of poverty for 1,623 municipalities and cities for the reference year 2000. The PSA thereafter produced small area estimates of poverty for 2003, 2006, and 2009, through various projects financed by the World Bank and the Government of Australia. The Government of the Philippines subsequently supported the generation of small area estimates for 2012 and 2015. This statistical activity is included in the Philippine Statistical Development Program, which highlights priority statistical development programs and activities that are meant to ensure the availability of essential information for national development planning and international commitments.

The poverty mapping approach merges expenditure or income variables from surveys with explanatory variables from censuses. An expenditure or income model is developed from survey data and applied to census data to generate household-level income or expenditure. This then serves as the input in calculating small area estimates of poverty and inequality (Das and Chambers 2015). In the Philippines, income models are constructed from the FIES and applied to Census of Population and Housing data to yield predicted income values. These predicted income values are compared with official poverty lines to generate the small area poverty estimates.

SAE methodologies, like conventional estimation methodologies, have limitations. The World Bank's poverty mapping methodology, for instance, requires that the survey and census data used to generate small area poverty estimates have consistent reference periods to ensure comparability of variables. One possible solution to this limitation is to restrict the explanatory variables in the estimation model to only those that do not vary over time, or those that are categorized as time invariant.

2.2   Enhancing Compilation of Development Statistics Through Big Data

Since SAE using survey and census data has its constraints, it is important to also explore other data sources in compiling development statistics. Research studies confirm that innovative data sources, such as big data, offer alternative inputs for enriching the estimation of development indicators (Eagle et al. 2010; Data 2x 2017). Compared to conventional data, it is also less expensive and more timely to access and compile information from big data. For instance, if telecommunication firms are open to sharing data, mobile phone data is far less costly to collect than household survey data. Mobile phone and satellite imagery can also provide real-time or more up-to-date data (Pizatella-Haswell 2018). If the goal is to produce more disaggregated data, broadening the SAE framework to include big data is a feasible approach (Box 2.1).

Box 2.1: Harmonizing Big Data in the Small Area Estimation Framework

Big data can play a role in the small area estimation (SAE) framework in three ways: first, examine big data variables to see if they have a strong relationship with the desired SAE variables; second, use big data variables as additional explanatory variables in SAE regression models; and third, use survey data to assess and remove bias associated with nonprobability sampling in big data (Marchetti et al. 2015).

Big data sources can readily provide data at the small-area level because such data are easy to collect and generate. However, self-selection bias is commonly associated with big data. To resolve this concern, big data values should be correlated with the desired SAE values. If there is a strong correlation, then it is safe to use big data for benchmarking information at the small-area level. However, if there is a low correlation, further research on other potential big data variables must be explored.

Big data variables can also serve as auxiliary variables in SAE regression modeling. The conventional SAE methodology integrates survey data with auxiliary data from census and administrative records. Today, the auxiliary variables can be expanded to include big data variables from satellite imagery, geospatial data, or mobile phone data—all of which can reflect socioeconomic conditions at more granular levels. However, employing big data variables in SAE modeling may entail a more advanced SAE methodology to address technical issues (e.g., sampling and nonsampling errors) in big data.

Another potential way to address self-selection bias in big data is to examine the consistency and reliability of big data against conventional survey data. To check for consistency, the distribution of values that are available in both big data sources and surveys can be compared. The differences in big data values and survey data values can then be used as inputs to estimate weights to lower the self-selection bias.

Source: S. Marchetti et al. 2015. Small Area Model-Based Estimators Using Big Data Sources. *Journal of Official Statistics*. 31 (2).pp. 263–281.

3 Tapping Computer Vision Algorithms for Predicting Poverty Rates

3.1   Introduction to Machine Learning Algorithms

Artificial intelligence, machine learning, and deep learning are terms that are often used interchangeably, but they differ from each other in some fundamental ways (Figure 3.1).

Artificial intelligence is a broad term referring to the creation of machines that are capable of simulating human intelligence in performing different tasks and solving problems. Apple's virtual personal assistant, Siri, is a famous application of artificial intelligence.

Machine learning, meanwhile, is a subfield of artificial intelligence. It allows machines to learn from data progressively and independently, without being explicitly programmed to do so (Goodfellow et al. 2016). To better understand the concept of machine learning, think about a child learning how to speak and read. Parents constantly talk to their child and give him or her books to read, progressing from simple to more complex ones over time. In this way, a child is given a lot of data to learn from (ADB 2020).

Figure 3.1: Comparing Definitions of Artificial Intelligence Frameworks

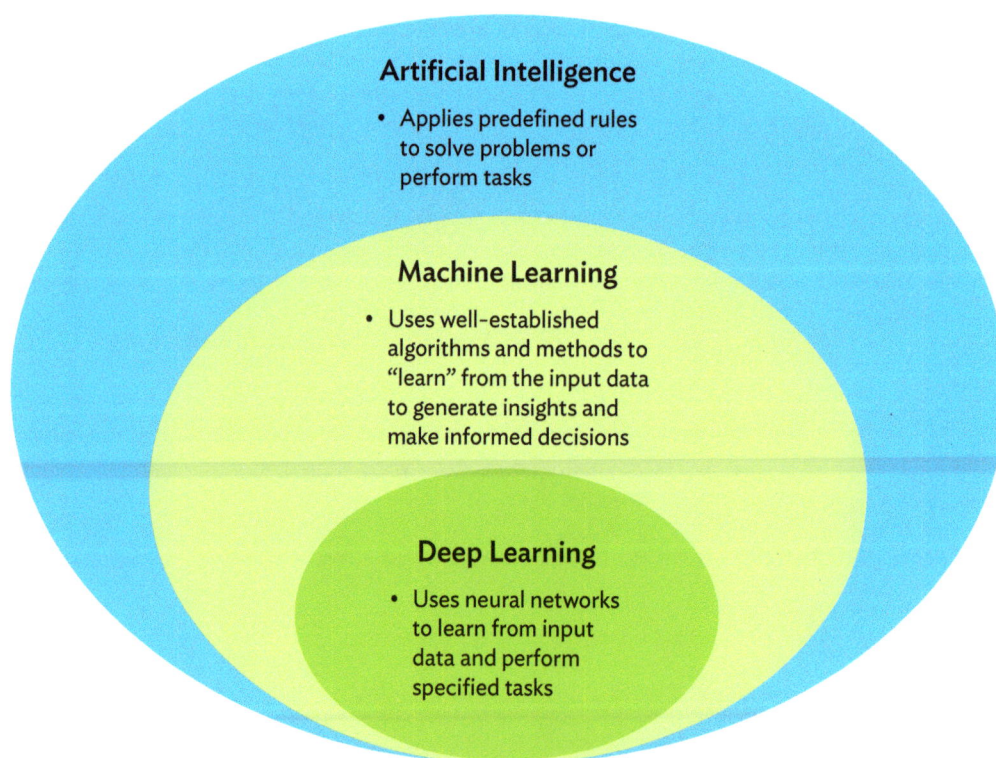

Artificial Intelligence
- Applies predefined rules to solve problems or perform tasks

Machine Learning
- Uses well-established algorithms and methods to "learn" from the input data to generate insights and make informed decisions

Deep Learning
- Uses neural networks to learn from input data and perform specified tasks

Source: F. Chollet. 2017. Deep Learning with Python. Manning. ISBN: 9781617294433.

Put simply, machine learning feeds an algorithm a lot of data and lets it figure things out on its own (ADB 2020). Machine learning is often based on well-established algorithms and methods, such as Decision Trees, Support Vector Machines, the Naive Bayes Classifier, and Logistic Regression. These algorithms are used to analyze the input data and "learn" from it in order to generate insights and inform decisions. The process usually requires complex mathematical calculations and heavy coding to get to the desired outcome. Among the popular examples of machine learning applications are Facebook's face recognition technology and the spam e-mail detection provided by Gmail and Hotmail.

Over time, machine learning algorithms have become increasingly sophisticated and capable of doing more complicated tasks, to a point where they now mimic the structure of the human brain (ADB 2020). This is the idea behind neural networks.

Deep learning is a broad term for machine learning procedures that follow a systematic structure patterned to reflect the human brain's natural decision-making processes (Goodfellow et al. 2016). Computer vision is an area of deep learning that shows the computer's ability to interpret patterns from digital images.

Neural Networks

A type of machine learning that resembles the human brain is known as a neural network. Similar to typical machine learning models, a neural network can learn various tasks on its own. It can simulate how the human brain solves problems by gathering inputs, processing them, and generating an output. A neural network can handle sophisticated tasks, such as text classification and categorization, machine translation, speech and character recognition, image recognition, and stock predictions.

Like the human brain, a neural network is made up of interconnected neurons or nodes and edges. A node represents a variable or a mathematical function connected by edges (ADB 2020). The interconnected nodes and edges, which contain an activation function, can be best illustrated through computational graphs (Figure 3.2).

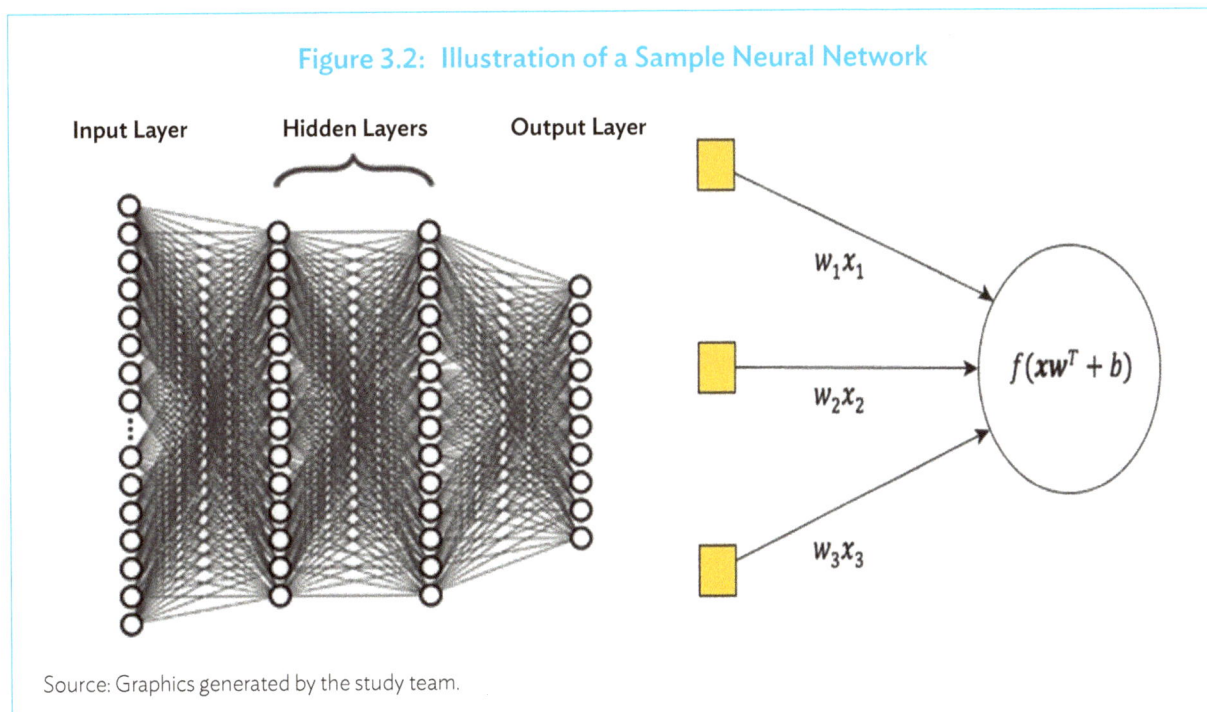

Figure 3.2: Illustration of a Sample Neural Network

Source: Graphics generated by the study team.

Figure 3.3 demonstrates the power of a neural network in performing a computer vision task. The first image clearly illustrates the handwritten digit "3". The computer, however, behaves differently than the human eye. While it can only look at obscure features of the images, it can be trained to detect detailed patterns. The second and third images explain how a machine learning algorithm works in filtering the images to identify geometric patterns, i.e., horizontal, vertical, orthogonal, and rotated features. Screening basic geometric features, e.g., edges and shapes, is the preliminary stage of the deep-learning algorithm. More intricate features can be classified as the deep-learning procedure advances to the point of being able to correctly assign detailed features into specific groups.

Figure 3.3: How a Computer Detects Features in a Vision Task

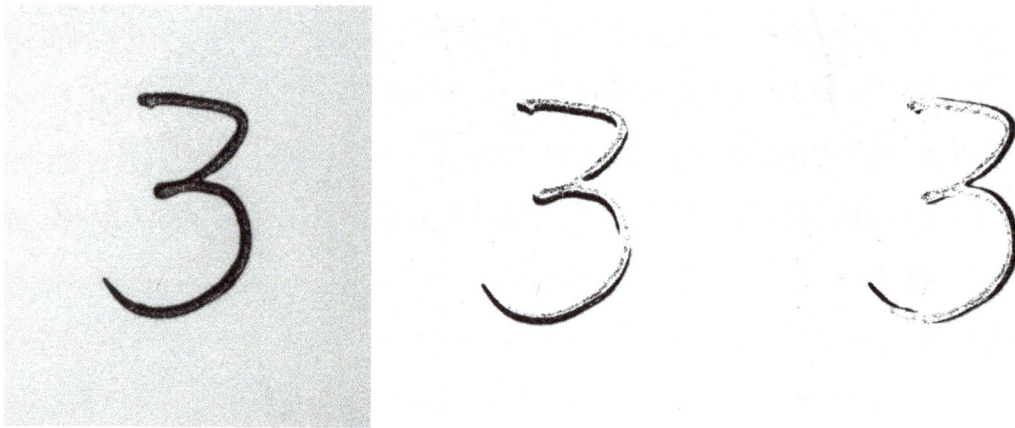

Source: Computer vision generated by the study team.

Many "labelled" images are needed for preparing an algorithm to correctly detect certain features. To recognize digit and letter patterns in particular, an algorithm requires training on a substantial number of labelled images with varying alphanumeric sequences—and this is where a neural network comes in.

A neural network consists of three types of layers – input, hidden, and output. The input layer receives the initial data. In the case of a computer vision task, the input layer refers to data from a digital image. The hidden layer has neurons that function as filters and are triggered whenever they recognize a distinct feature or particular arrangement of edges or shapes. The output layer provides the correct classification of the feature.

How a neural network functions can be explained using a handwritten numeric character, which can be transformed into digital layout. Figure 3.4 illustrates a sample neural network that can detect an input image representing the number "3". Consider that the digital image is designed as an 8 x 8 pixel image. The neural network's input layer therefore starts with 64 neurons, matching each of the 8 x 8 pixels.

In the input layer, every neuron has a corresponding numerical value that is associated with the pixel's grayscale values. Grayscale values normally range from 0 to 1, where black is 0 and white is 1. In the hidden layer, these values are converted into mathematical expressions that can detect distinct features of an image. The neurons in the hidden layer are activated based on the numerical values. For this illustration, a lower number causes the neuron to "light up", indicating a distinct pattern. In Figure 3.4, there are two hidden layers that filter specific patterns. The first layer searches for horizontal patterns, while the second layer searches for vertical patterns before classifying the detail into one of the 10 numerical digits in the output layer. In the output

Figure 3.4: Illustration of a Neural Network

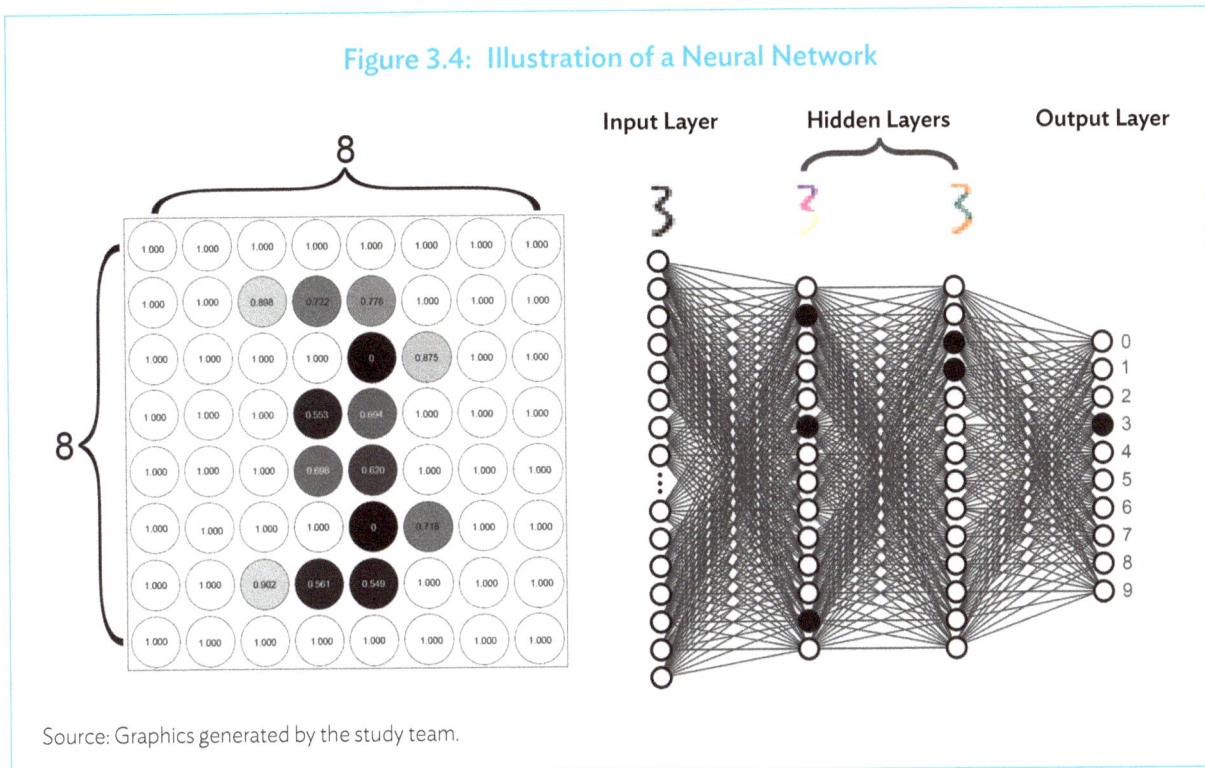

Source: Graphics generated by the study team.

layer, activation of the neurons reveals the extent to which the neural network recognizes the input image of a numerical digit.

Convolutional Neural Networks

A neural network can be classified into different types, depending on the parameters and principles used in determining its outputs. A convolutional neural network (CNN) is a type of neural network that can perform image classification and computer vision tasks. Figure 3.5 demonstrates how a CNN works using the same example as in Figure 3.4. Suppose there are four 3 pixel x 3 pixel filters on the first row of the neural network, where each filter is designed to find different image features, i.e., a type of edge or line. The first filter looks for top horizontal edges as indicated by the brightest pixel, while the second filter looks for left vertical edges. The third and fourth filters look for bottom horizontal edges and right vertical edges, respectively (ADB 2020).

Mathematically, each filter generates values, where each value is equivalent to a particular color, i.e., –1s for black, 1s for white, and 0s for gray, and therefore describes a specific characteristic of the feature. Using its convolutional layers, the CNN works by organizing these values to find patterns and characteristics within the image. The input image, in this example, is the image of a "3". During the convolution, an individual filter looks at every group of 9 pixels that are clustered next to each other. As the filter goes deeper into the CNN, the layers are able to detect more sophisticated patterns. Visually, the output of this process appears similar to the third row of Figure 3.5.

Consistent with the majority of neural network types, the CNN is programmed to handle the large volumes of unstructured, pixelized data found in digital images. However, compared with other neural network variants, the CNN is more mathematically capable of filtering significant image features without requiring human intervention (Yamashita et al. 2018). CNNs are also more popular for image recognition functions because they can be executed—through special convolution, pooling operations, and parameter sharing—in practically any instrument (Dai et al. 2020; Yamashita et al. 2018).

Figure 3.5: Neural Network Filters to Detect Vertical and Horizontal Lines

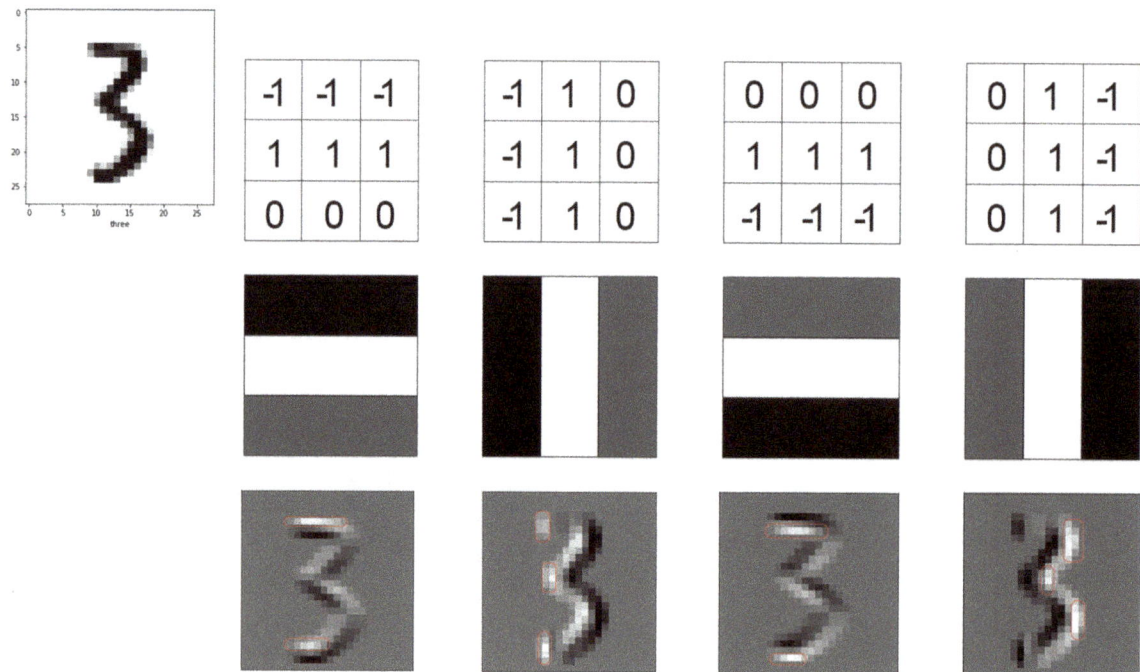

Source: Graphics generated by the study team: based on a YouTube videos by 3blue1brown entitled "But what is a Neural Network? | Deep learning chapter 1"; and Deeplizard entitled "Convolutional Neural Networks (CNN) explained."

Loss Functions

The loss function is a vital element of machine learning because it provides an indication of how effective an algorithm executes the input data. It is synonymous with predicting errors in regression models. Since the loss function generates a large value if predicted values are significantly different from actual values, the objective is to minimize the loss function value.

Loss functions are generally classified into two variants, based on the kind of learning tasks: regression losses and classification losses. Regression loss functions cover the prediction of continuous values, e.g., prediction of expenditure, income. Typical examples of regression loss functions are "mean square errors" and "mean absolute errors". Classification loss functions, on the other hand, deal with predicting categorical values, e.g., to assess images of alphanumeric digits and group them into one of 0–9 digits. The cross entropy loss function, which determines the performance of an algorithm whose output is a probability value between 0 and 1, is conventionally adopted in classification-related tasks. Figure 3.6 shows how cross entropy loss functions return higher values as the predicted probability deviates from the actual label (ADB 2020).

Confusion Matrixes

Aside from using loss functions, producing a "confusion matrix" or "error matrix" can also assess the performance of a machine learning algorithm assigned to classification-related tasks. The confusion matrix is a table showing different combinations of machine learning predicted values and the actual values. It lays out the frequency of values of machine learning predicted classification versus the frequency of values of actual classification. In the example of Table 3.1, there are 100 images representing numerical digits "4", "5", and "6". The far right column

Figure 3.6: Measuring Cross Entropy Loss against Predicted Probability

Log loss when true label = 1

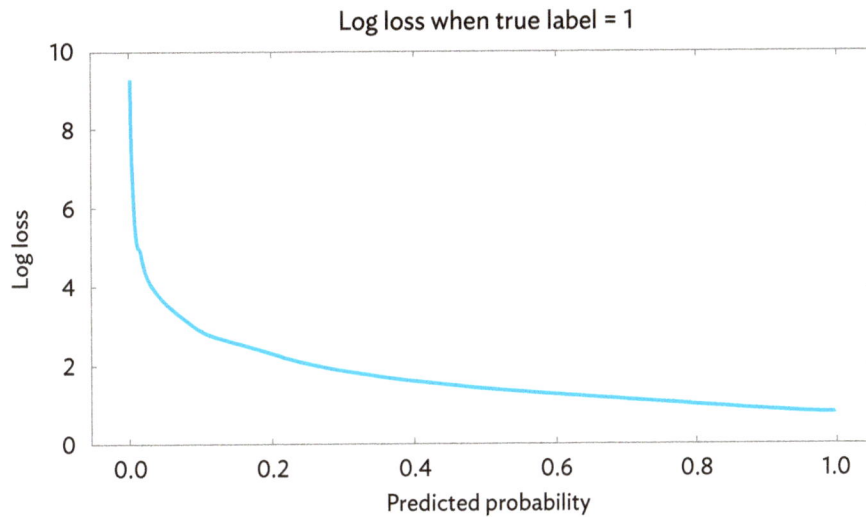

Source: Calculations and graphics generated by the study team.

Table 3.1: Sample Confusion Matrix

Machine learning-predicted class

		4	5	6	# images to be classified
Actual class	**4**	48	8	4	60
	5	3	20	2	25
	6	1	2	12	15
	# images classified	52	30	18	100

Source: Calculations generated by the study team.

corresponds to the number of images of "4", "5", and "6" that should be classified, while the columns to the left represent the number of images classified as "4", "5", and "6" by the machine learning algorithm. In this case, out of 60 images of "4", 48 have been correctly classified, while eight images were misclassified as "5" and four images were misclassified as "6".

Other Key Concepts

Optimization. Optimization is a method for improving the algorithm's performance. It begins with assigning some kind of loss function and ends with changing model parameters to minimize the assigned loss function.

Epoch. In machine learning, an epoch indicates one cycle completed by the training data set. A majority of machine learning algorithms require several epochs for the learning process.

Learning Rate. Learning rates are essential in training a deep-learning model. To minimize the loss functions, learning rates set the degree of change in parameters.

Plotting the learning rate against the loss function can measure the range of the learning rate (Figure 3.7a). The learning range can start from the smallest loss (1e-6) and graduate to the point where the graph begins to ascend (1e-04) to prevent an increase. Suppose that there are only three layers in the neural network. The first layers would train at a learning rate equivalent to 1e-6, the second layer at 1e-5, and the last layer at 1e-4. Frameworks normally split the network's layers into groups and train them at various learning rates. This process refers to discriminative learning.

Figure 3.7b illustrates another case of selecting a learning rate before the minimum loss value, which is the range where the loss is still decreasing or anything between 1e-2 and 1e-1. This is employed to train the model's last layer.

The following terms explain core concepts related to executing deep-learning algorithms and frameworks based on the Python computer programming language. Python is an advanced, general-purpose programming language that is widely recognized by machine learning and data science practitioners.

Prototyping. This refers to developing a small-scale running version of a program. Deep learning is often used to address the three defining properties of big data, i.e., volume, velocity, and variety. There are therefore merits in finding a deep-learning framework that can be easily established for this purpose.

Computational graph. Math functions are explained in graph theory like a flowchart for functions. Computational graphs are essential to direct learning frameworks for the optimization of the model through the adjustments of weights and biases. These also allow parallelism to make training fast and efficient. There are two types of computational graphs – static and dynamic. Static graphs are used when the inputs are of the same size. It is defined

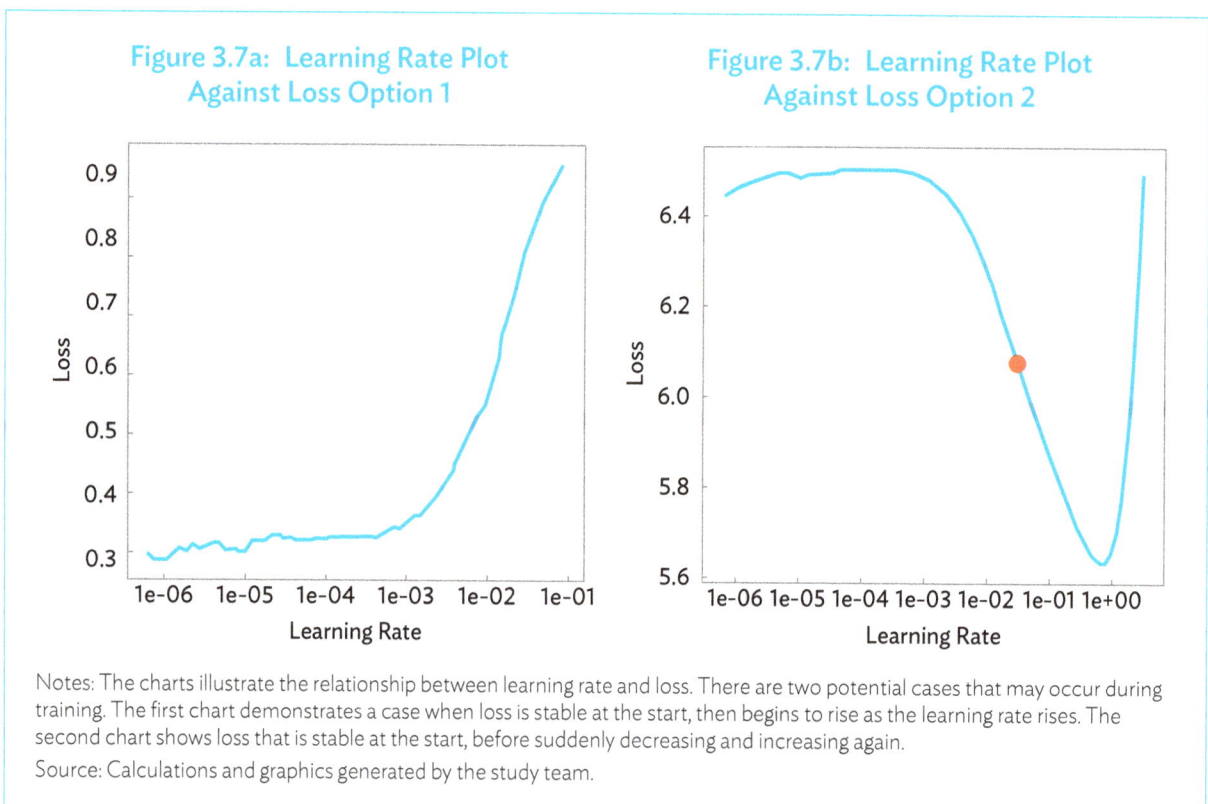

Figure 3.7a: Learning Rate Plot Against Loss Option 1

Figure 3.7b: Learning Rate Plot Against Loss Option 2

Notes: The charts illustrate the relationship between learning rate and loss. There are two potential cases that may occur during training. The first chart demonstrates a case when loss is stable at the start, then begins to rise as the learning rate rises. The second chart shows loss that is stable at the start, before suddenly decreasing and increasing again.
Source: Calculations and graphics generated by the study team.

before the model training starts and can be used to schedule computations across multiple computing device for a shared computational cost. Static graphs are immutable; thus, nodes cannot be altered at runtime. Dynamic graphs on the other hand, are particularly useful when the input data varies in size like training in natural language processing. In this case, graphs are created after each training iterations and nodes can be altered during runtime.

Learning curve. One advantageous feature of Python is its concise and readable codes, which are easy to learn. It is simple to understand a deep-learning framework when it adopts Python's coding style, commonly known as "Pythonic" code. Python enables developers to easily build models for machine learning.

Production and scalability. After training a deep-learning model, the next step is production. The model is incorporated into the available software, website, or mobile application for adoption by clients. If the objective is to distribute the research afterward, a deep-learning framework with deployment solutions can be chosen.

Scalability, which takes place in the hardware and deep-learning framework, pertains to the efficiency and effectiveness of managing tremendous volumes of data at high computational speeds during training. It may refer to the framework's support for distributed or parallelized training, by splitting the model computations to different devices (model parallelism) and dividing the data into modules processed separately by different devices (data parallelism).

Community and resources. Like other scientific frameworks, machine learning has an online global community consisting of users and developers that contribute to the improvement of the framework. A large community offers wider resources for sharing new algorithms, new data sources, and new discoveries in the field.

TensorFlow and PyTorch are two emerging and widely utilized frameworks (based on the number of job listings requiring knowledge of these software packages, Google web searches, project development activities in Github, and web articles published in Medium, ArXiv, and Quora). Both packages are nonproprietary deep-learning software options, designed by Google (TensorFlow) and Facebook (PyTorch). The study team also recognized the prominence of Keras and Fastai, which are application programming interfaces that can be executed in TensorFlow and PyTorch, respectively (Table 3.2).

Fastai and PyTorch are deep-learning libraries that offer high-level components to efficiently produce advanced results in standard deep-learning domains for experts. These deep-learning libraries also offer low-level components that can be combined to develop new approaches for researchers.

3.2   Estimating Poverty Rates Using Satellite Imagery and Geospatial Data

Now that the concepts of deep-learning have been established, particularly in the context of image-classification tasks, it is possible to discuss how such technology can be applied to using big data, particularly satellite imagery, as an alternative source of data inputs in poverty estimation.

A Quick Review of Existing Literature

Existing studies suggest two approaches to predicting poverty using innovative data sources.

The first approach requires building a structural model for estimating poverty, using explanatory variables from geospatial and other satellite imagery-related sources. In Sri Lanka, a World Bank study developed a model using auxiliary variables derived from satellite imagery—e.g., building density and number, shadow areas, car counts, road density, farmland types, roof materials, and vegetation index—in predicting poverty at the village level. The study's findings revealed an association between these geospatial variables and resulting poverty estimates, with the model explaining about 40%–60% of variability in poverty at the granular level (Engstrom, Hersch, and Newhouse 2016).

Table 3.2: Comparison of Common Deep-Learning Software Frameworks

	TensorFlow	PyTorch
Prototyping	In the latest version 2.0, TensorFlow has adopted eager execution, an imperative programming environment that allows for faster prototyping.	Fast prototyping using imperative programming.
Computational graphs	Uses static computational graphs A library called TensorFlow Fold can be used for creating TensorFlow models using dynamic batching to create static graphs that emulate dynamic graphs.	Uses built-in dynamic computational graphs.
Learning curve	Uses less Pythonic coding, which is not so simple for beginners.	Uses Pythonic coding and is therefore easy to learn.
Community and resources	A mature framework with a broad user community and many projects, tutorials, and training modules, and other resources.	A younger framework, also with a good community and resources.
Production and scalability	Production-ready using TensorFlow serving and with easy mobile and embedded device support using TensorFlow Lit. Features data and model parallelism for ease of scalability. Better for large scale deployments.	Better used in research, hobby, and small projects. Needs an API server for production. Simpler distributed training implementation.

Sources: Information compiled by the study team, using various sources (Exxact Corporation 2019; Hannun 2017; Hutchins et al. 2020; Kurama 2020).

In Tuscany, Italy, another model, using mobility information from global positioning system sources as auxiliary variables, predicted the number of poor people and the average household income at the local labor system level (Marchetti et al. 2015).

The second approach to predicting poverty using innovative data sources is less structured and depends on deep-learning techniques. In India, a study team implemented a convolutional model using conventional housing variables (i.e., roof materials, light sources, drinking water sources) and satellite imagery variables (i.e., roads, farms, bodies of water) to estimate income and poverty levels (Pandey et al. 2018). Meanwhile, a study covering several North American cities and one South American city— Boston, Chicago, Houston, Los Angeles, and Philadelphia, in the United States; and Santiago in Chile—also predicted poverty through machine learning algorithms (Piaggesi et al. 2019).

Although more abstract, the second approach is widely seen to provide more accurate predictions of poverty. Stanford University research on machine learning, which followed the second approach, is one of the most cited references using deep learning to predict poverty (Jean et al. 2016).

Predicting Poverty Using Satellite Imagery

Analyzing all elements of satellite images and comparing these elements with poverty levels is deemed challenging because of the highly unstructured state of the images. Using a robust algorithm that systematizes poverty prediction for geographic areas can vastly improve this strategy.

Poverty data and daytime satellite imagery can potentially be directly connected to a computer vision approach to generate optimum results. In most instances, however, this is not feasible because the labelled data that identify certain characteristics or classifications of poverty are scarce in the poverty estimation framework. Many statistical offices generate official poverty statistics only at highly aggregated levels, i.e., national, regional, or provincial. Other countries employ traditional SAE methodologies to release poverty data at more granular levels, e.g., municipality or village level. Even so, a country with 2,000 municipalities and 2,000 corresponding poverty-labelled images may be insufficient for an algorithm to accurately estimate poverty.

In other words, poverty data are often not available at the sufficiently disaggregated levels required for training a large algorithm. A typical deep-learning technique for analyzing imagery works well only with a vast number, say millions, of labelled images for training (Krizhevsky et al. 2012).

The Stanford study (Jean et al. 2016) implemented three areas of artificial intelligence: machine learning, deep learning, and computer vision. This method entails preparing an algorithm that can execute a vision-based task, e.g., using daytime satellite imagery to predict the intensity of night lights. The study suggests a transfer-learning technique that starts with developing a trained algorithm for measuring night light intensity, instead of directly preparing an algorithm for measuring poverty. Night light intensity can serve as proxy indicator for economic growth, on the premise that highly developed areas are well lit at night as compared with undeveloped areas. Other literature also suggests a high correlation of nighttime luminosity with metrics of economic development and population growth (Zhou et al. 2015; Akiyama 2012; Ghosh et al. 2010; Amaral et al. 2006; Lo 2001; Sutton 1997).

Night light data are more readily available and can provide more disaggregated data than conventional poverty data. Hence, it is more beneficial to develop a trained algorithm for predicting night light intensity than a trained algorithm for predicting poverty directly. The trained algorithm can learn to detect many features that a human eye can also identify, including infrastructure (e.g., roads and bridges), vehicles, and farmland areas recognized by nighttime luminosity. The Stanford study (2016) suggests that, as soon as the algorithm is trained to match an image's feature with a specific night light intensity, the learning can be transferred to predict poverty.

Data Requirements in the Philippine Poverty Mapping Study

The case study conducted by ADB, the PSA, and the World Data Lab applied the Stanford methodology to measuring poverty across the Philippines. This entailed the following data requirements:

Daytime Satellite Imagery. Daytime satellite imagery is the first data input to the poverty estimation methodology used in this study. Satellite imagery can be sourced from different repositories offering different resolutions and forms of availability, i.e., some are publicly available, while others are exclusive to paying clients, i.e., proprietary datasets (Box 3.1).

The Stanford research used Google Static Maps with 2-meter (m) resolutions, which are proprietary datasets. NSOs that intend to use this methodology are encouraged to use publicly available satellite images with lower resolution. Doing so will be within the reach of the resources available to many NSOs, and will enable them to evaluate whether or not lower resolution images can provide acceptable results despite constraints on image resolution.

This poverty mapping study used nonproprietary, georeferenced, and tagged image files from Landsat 7 and 8 with 15 m resolution (enhanced from 30 m), and from Sentinel 2 with 10 m resolution. Landsat data were used for 2012 and 2013, while Sentinel data covered later years. Images from "2015-10-01" to "2016-12-31" were used for 2015 because Sentinel imagery is only accessible from October 2015 (using images for only the last quarter of 2015 would not be adequate to generate a full country composite, considering the limitations of cloud cover). For Landsat years, 256-pixel x 256-pixel images were used because they worked better for CNN training. These images provided a grid size of 3,840 m (15 m x 256 pixels) at the equator. For Sentinel years, 384-pixel x 384-pixel images were used to reproduce the same grid for all years. This produced about 13,000 images.

Box 3.1: What Are Different Sources of Earth Observations?

There are three categories of Earth orbit satellite system, arranged according to altitude: low Earth orbit (LEO), medium Earth orbit (MEO), and geostationary (GEO) satellites (United Nations 2017).

LEO satellites have an altitude above the Earth's surface of between 400 kilometers (km) and 800 km. These satellites rotate over the Earth's poles at approximately 28,000 km per hour and can finish their orbit around the Earth in about 90 minutes. LEO satellites have better coverage of the poles at the equator and better spatial resolution because of their proximity to the ground. These satellites can provide a maximum of 30 centimeters per pixel resolution for black and white or panchromatic images and roughly 1 meter (m) per pixel resolution for colored or multispectral band images. Among the widely used and most accessible LEO satellites with established data and research applications are Moderate Resolution Imaging Spectroradiometer satellites with spatial resolutions of 250 m, 500 m, and 1000 m; Landsat sensors with spatial resolution of 30 m; and Sentinel-2A and 2B satellites, operated by the European Space Agency, with spatial resolutions of 10 m to 60 m.

MEO satellites have an altitude above Earth of about 20,000 km. These satellites are used for communication, navigation, and geodetic or space environment purposes.

GEO satellites are positioned at approximately 36,000 km above the Earth. They can remain stationary at a specific position. These satellites can provide better Earth surface coverage because of their high orbit, but the images produced can have increasingly skewed pixels toward the edges of the sensor coverage. GEO satellites are primarily developed for meteorological reasons. The Himawari-8 satellite, which is stationed over Indonesia, is one example of a GEO satellite. It has 50% coverage of the Earth and has a spatial resolution of 500 m for images captured every 10 minutes.

A conventional satellite is packed with many sensors for various types of observations. Landsat 8, for instance, has the greatest number of spectral bands (11) in the Landsat series, where each band serves a particular purpose.

Uses of Landsat 8 Spectral Bands

Band	Wavelength	Purpose
Band 1—coastal aerosol	0.43–0.45	Coastal and aerosol studies.
Band 2—blue	0.45–0.51	Bathymetric mapping, differentiating soil from vegetation and deciduous from coniferous vegetation.
Band 3—green	0.53–0.59	Features peak vegetation, which is useful for assessing plant vigor and total suspended matter in water bodies.
Band 4—red	0.64–0.67	Distinguishes vegetation spectral slopes; also measures the primary photosynthetic pigment in plants (terrestrial and aquatic) chlorophyll-a.
Band 5—Near Infrared	0.85–0.88	Highlights biomass content and shorelines.
Band 6—Short-wave Infrared 1	1.57–1.65	Distinguishes moisture content of soil and vegetation; penetrates thin clouds.
Band 7—Short-wave Infrared 2	2.11–2.29	Enhance moisture content of soil and vegetation and thin cloud penetration.
Band 8—Panchromatic	0.50–0.68	15-meter resolution, sharper image definition.
Band 9—Cirrus	1.36–1.38	Enhance detection of cirrus cloud contamination.
Band 10—Thermal Infrared Sensor 1	10.60–11.19	100-meter resolution, thermal mapping and estimated soil moisture.
Band 11—Thermal Infrared Sensor 2	11.5–12.51	100-meter resolution, improved thermal mapping and estimated soil moisture.

Source: United Nations. 2017. Earth Observations for Official Statistics: Satellite Imagery and Geospatial Data Task Team Report.

Figure 3.8: Image Color Bands within a Georeferenced Image File

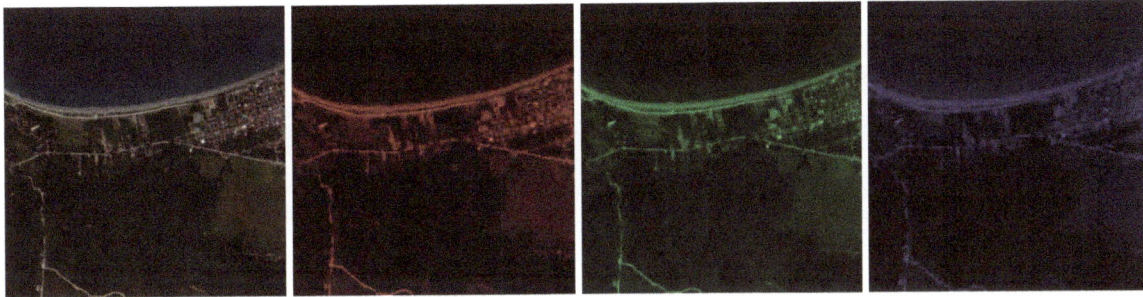

Note: These images were taken over the Philippines (Claveria, Cagayan).
Source: Sentinel 2 satellite.

The image files were saved as three-dimensional arrays, where every pixel is depicted in red, green, and blue (RGB) color bands (Figure 3.8).[16]

The center of each image was used as reference point when determining which province, city, or municipality the image was part of.

Preparation of the satellite images started with gathering daytime images without cloud obstruction for the whole of the Philippines. This approach required executing an algorithm to identify the most acceptable and cloud-free daytime images during the study's reference period. This was done through a series of tests until the algorithm yielded a pooled satellite image with minimal cloudiness.

Another preparatory step was image processing through pansharpening, which aims to enhance the resolution of Landsat 7 and 8 images. Figure 3.9 illustrates pansharpening of images, merging daytime satellite panchromatic images (black and white, but also color sensitive) and low-resolution multispectral band RGB images to generate multiband RGB images with higher resolution. The process involves upsampling or increasing the amount of pixel per unit area of the multispectral band RGB image, converting the RGB color scheme into hue saturation value, and replacing the value with the pixel intensity of the panchromatic image. After pansharpening, the Landsat image resolution was enhanced to 15 m from the initial 30 m resolution.

A number of validation checks were also done during the training process. These included assessing images with low quality due to cloudiness or unrecognizable land areas, which rendered the highest loss, then isolating these images to prevent contamination of the input dataset. Higher levels of loss during the early training process indicates that the algorithm is doing well in detecting appropriate features in the satellite images. Figure 3.10 shows examples of images with high prediction loss, i.e., very cloudy conditions with no recognizable land or urban areas, which could render the model inaccurate in predicting class and training correct features. The poor quality of these images was caused either by weather disturbances or technical problems with the satellite sensor. They were eliminated from further training.

Data augmentation was also implemented to avoid model overfitting. This concept is used for daytime imagery to obtain additional samples in the training dataset. It helps create a model that generalizes better and minimizes imbalanced classes in the dataset. The data augmentation techniques applied were vertical and horizontal flipping,

---

[16] Satellites generally have numerous and often varied bands. This study, however, concentrated on RGB color bands, since the CNN was pretrained on regular RGB images through ImageNet.

Figure 3.9: Pansharpening to Improve Image Resolution

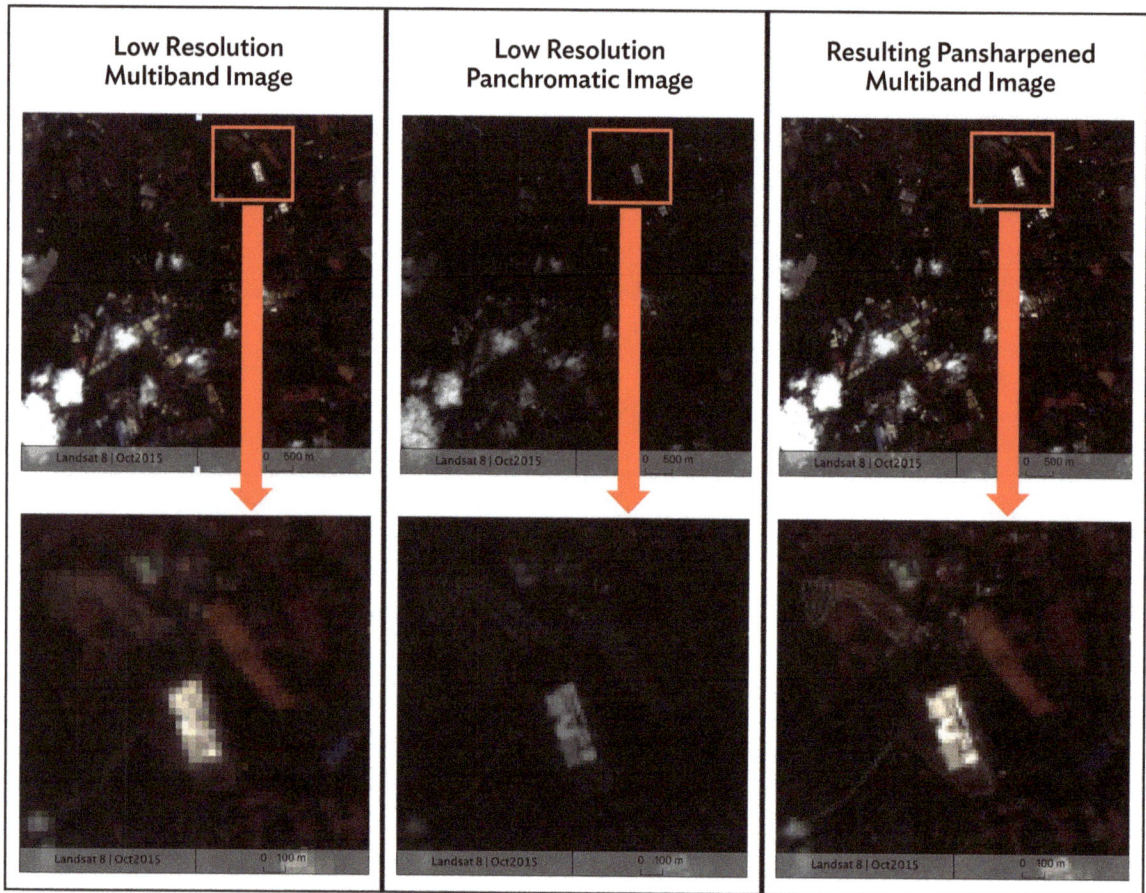

Note: These images were taken over Biñan City and Sta. Rosa City, Laguna, Philippines.
Source: Landsat 8 via Google Earth Engine.

Figure 3.10: Low-Quality Satellite Images Isolated from Training

Note: These images were captured over Laguna Lake in the Philippines.
Source: Landsat 8 satellite.

random lighting and contrast changes with 10% probability, and dihedral and symmetric warping, all of which are suitable for remote-sensing images (Perez and Wang 2017).

Google Earth Engine was the platform used in most of the data preparation stages of this study. It combines a multipetabyte catalogue of satellite imagery and geospatial datasets with planetary-scale analysis capabilities. Additionally, the Geospatial Data Abstraction Library was used to crop images and convert them into a proper geospatial data format. This library is an open-source computer software translator library for raster and vector geospatial data formats.

Data on Night Lights. The second set of data input for this study was information on intensity of night lights. These data were sourced from the Visible Infrared Imaging Radiometer Suite (VIIRS) instrument, which compiles downloadable global earth observations of nighttime images (Figure 3.11). For the lit areas, the cloud-free average radiance value of the nighttime images was used and preprocessed to eliminate ephemeral lights caused by fires and other similar events. The unlit areas, on the other hand, were assigned zero values.

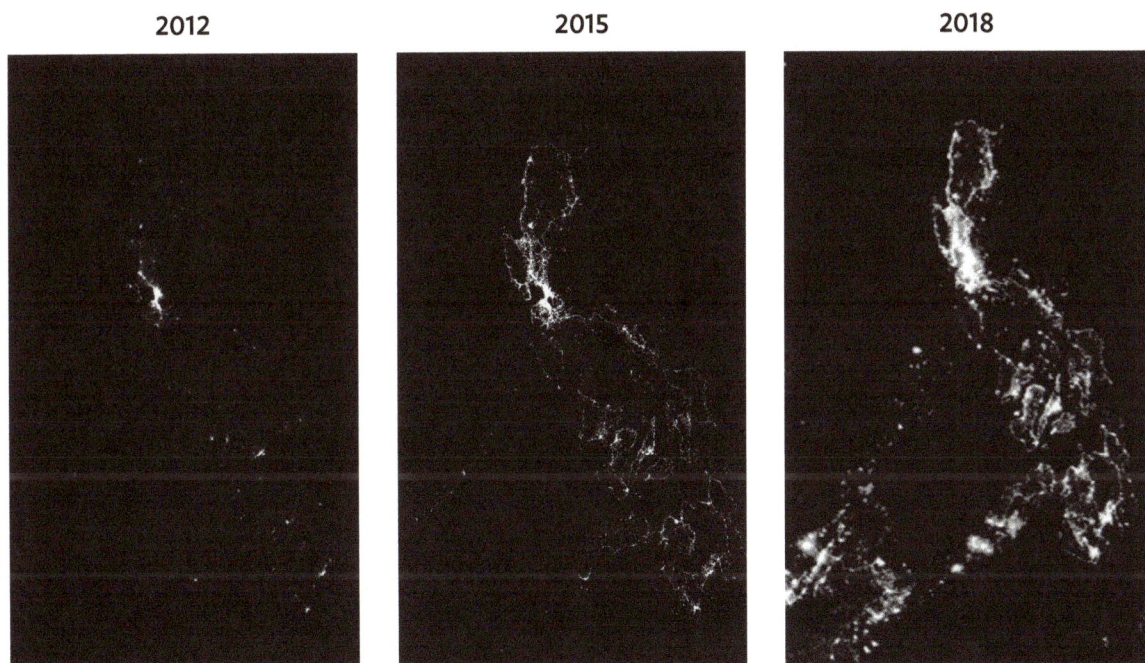

Figure 3.11: Examples of Nighttime Light Image Tiles

| 2012 | 2015 | 2018 |

Note: These images show the annual composite distribution of night lights in the Philippines.
Source: Visible Infrared Imaging Radiometer Suite.

VIIRS provides publicly available composite images that are released monthly, but for some years they also provide annual composite images. For this study, custom year composite images were generated for consistency with the goal of estimating annual poverty statistics for the selected years. The median of the monthly data was calculated to reduce the effect of extreme values. Further refinements of the data were also carried out to ensure that night light resolution was consistent with daytime satellite resolution—a prerequisite to CNN modeling.

This study also followed the Stanford approach of clustering the actual night light intensity values into discrete groups, which facilitates a more effective training of the CNN model. Additionally, a Gaussian mixture model

Table 3.3: Nighttime Light Clusters in the Philippines

Year	Type	Class 1	Class 2	Class 3
2012	Manual	nl <= 0.15	1.0 >=nl > 0.15	nl > 1.0
2015	Manual	nl <= 0.16	1.5 >=nl > 0.16	nl >1.5
2018	Manual	nl <= 0.28	1.125 >=nl > 0.28	nl >1.125

nl= night lights
Source: Calculations generated by the study team.

(GMM) for clustering of night light intensity values was developed (Table 3.3). The GMM basically contends that the distribution of night light intensity results from the mixture of k underlying Normal or Gaussian distributions. The histogram of the radiance values was analyzed to identify the set of Normal distribution that conforms with the data.[17]

Poverty Statistics. Poverty statistics, a key welfare indicator,[18] were the third data input for this study. In the Philippines, small area poverty estimates were generated using the poverty mapping methodology of the World Bank, otherwise known as the Elbers, Lanjouw, and Lanjouw methodology (2003). Income models for Filipino households were built from survey datasets and applied to census datasets to yield predicted income values. These predicted income values, together with official poverty lines, served as inputs in generating poverty estimates at the municipality and city level.[19] The 2012 and 2015 small area poverty estimates for more than 1,600 municipalities and cities[20], and the 2018 official poverty estimates[21] from the Family Income and Expenditure Survey (FIES) for 81 provinces, were used as reference points in this case study (Figure 3.12).

Since the barangay (village) is the smallest geographical unit in the Philippines, followed by municipality and city, the published small area poverty estimates are not necessarily the most disaggregated, but further refinement may reduce the reliability of these estimates (especially for municipalities and cities with already high coefficients of variation). It should be noted, however, that estimates generated at the barangay level could contribute to even better data analysis and more effective targeting of policy initiatives to reduce poverty.

The 2012 and 2015 municipality and city poverty estimates, and the 2018 provincial poverty estimates, will be collectively described as government-published estimates in the succeeding discussions.

---

[17] The GMM approach does not always ensure correct outcomes. There are instances when this approach fails to generate optimal clusters. When this happens, researchers aim to identify optimal cluster through heuristic approaches or experimentation. It is also necessary to generate clusters such that the smallest cluster has at least a few hundred values, otherwise the data would be insufficient when these are split for training and validation. For this case study, three clusters were formed.

[18] In the Stanford study, which used data from African countries, data on village-level mean consumption expenditure were derived from the Living Standards Measurement Survey, and household assets score from the Demographic and Health Survey (Jean et al. 2016). However, official household surveys in the Philippines do not provide reliable estimates at the village level.

[19] In the case of the Philippines, per capita household income, which is the variable of interest regarding poverty, is available from the FIES. Auxiliary variables from the FIES, the Labor Force Survey, and the Census of Population and Housing are combined to build a per capita income model in log terms. The survey-obtainable explanatory variables refer to household or individual level variables such as educational attainment of household head, while census-derivable explanatory variables refer to municipal or barangay means, such as average family size in the barangay. The covariates in the regression model are strategically chosen such that they have comparable definitions, consistent summary statistics (such as mean values), and are available in both surveys and census. The predicted household per capita incomes are then compared with official provincial poverty lines to calculate the small area poverty estimates (PSA 2005, 2016). For the 2015 small area poverty estimates, the poverty rates range from 0.7% to 78.5%, while the coefficients of variation of resulting poverty estimates range from 2.9% to 55.5%.

[20] The area of municipalities or cities in the Philippines ranges from 3.0 million square meters (m^2) to 2.1 billion m^2, with a median size of 112.1 million m^2.

[21] Official poverty statistics in the Philippines are not based on small area estimates and are instead directly estimated from PSA surveys. Official poverty statistics are published at higher aggregation levels (i.e., national, regional, provincial, and highly urbanized cities). Poverty estimates at the province and highly urbanized city levels are the most granular numbers available for 2018, and their inclusion allows assessment of whether or not granularity of the indicator to be used for training CNN has an impact on the extent of granularity at which predictions can be made.

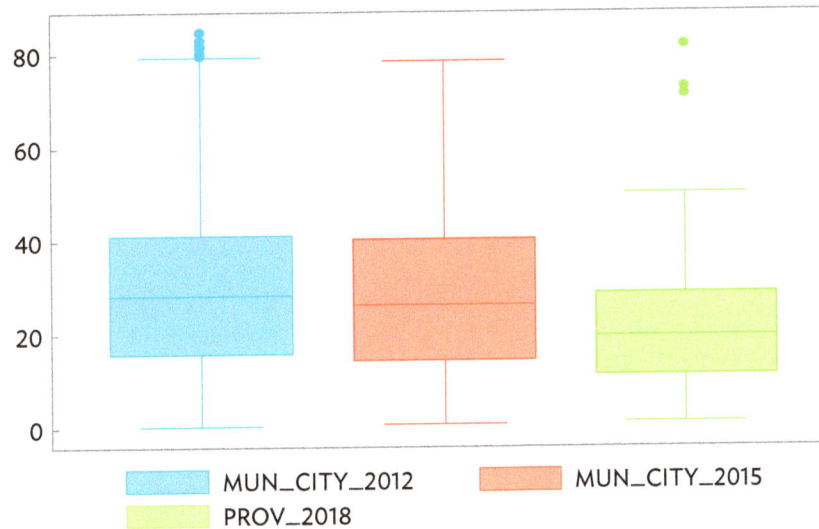

Figure 3.12: Geographical Distribution of Poverty Rates in the Philippines

Source: Calculations and graphics generated by the study team.

3.3   Training a Convolutional Neural Network to Predict Intensity of Night Lights

As already established, this poverty mapping study relies on an algorithm that can execute a vision-based task, e.g., using daytime satellite imagery to predict the intensity of night lights, with the latter being a proxy for poverty distribution. As part of an intermediate step, the algorithm had to be trained to categorize daytime satellite images into various clusters, with features related to various stages of economic development. Under this transfer-learning method, the task entailed teaching a CNN to predict nighttime luminosity relying on daytime satellite image features, then applying those features to predict poverty.[22]

To confirm if the algorithm could detect basic features, an off-the-shelf CNN (ResNet34), pretrained in the ImageNet database, was employed, rather than constructing a CNN algorithm from the start.[23]

Throughout the training process, various CNN specifications were implemented to determine the optimal network structure. Box 3.2 provides technical aspects of implementing and optimizing the CNN.

An alternative step to improve any CNN training process is to examine the confusion matrix, which provides the number of correct and incorrect predictions, and applies a proper loss function to reduce imbalanced prediction losses. Tables 3.4a and 3.4b display two illustrations of confusion matrices; one using a weighted cross entropy loss function, and one not using a weighted cross entropy loss function. The y-axis presents the number of images classified in each of the groups or bins generated according to the distribution of night light intensity. The x-axis

---

[22] Two cases of transfer-learning techniques were implemented. The first case employed a pretrained image classifier instead of random parameters in the CNN. The pretrained model was created on a large image database. The fundamental features of the initial layers (i.e., edges, corners, and other geometric features) are beneficial for whichever image classification type. Employing a CNN that had already learned to identify specific features can significantly minimize computing time.

[23] In pretraining, an existing algorithm that is trained in a variety of images and can therefore identify features including lines, edges, etc. was used. Several features that are important for general image classification tasks intersect, irrespective of the origin of the image. In this case, ImageNet is recognized a standard performer in running computer vision predictions.

presents the number of images predicted under each group. Correctly predicted images lie on the main diagonal and every other image on the off diagonal. Since the classes are ordinal, the first group is associated with low night light intensity, while the third group is associated with high night light intensity, being farther from the main diagonal indicates higher prediction error. A weighted cross entropy loss function was selected because, as Table 3.4a illustrates, this type of loss function penalizes the model more for wrong prediction of low frequency (3—high night light intensity) based on weights. Thus, this approach prevents the model from always predicting low nightlight classes because they have the most samples.

In this study, over 500 features were obtained from the final layer of the CNN. Figure 3.13 shows illustrations of these features and their correlation with the intensity of night lights. Fastai was used in implementing the CNN.

Table 3.4a: Sample Confusion Matrix with Weighted Cross Entropy Loss

		Predicted 1	2	3
Actual	1	1,299	24	2
	2	36	32	6
	3	4	12	21

Source: Calculations generated by the study team.

Table 3.4b: Sample Confusion Matrix without Weighted Cross Entropy Loss

		Predicted 1	2	3
Actual	1	2,384	9	2
	2	92	29	7
	3	14	11	30

Source: Calculations generated by the study team.

Figure 3.13: Examples of Features Derived from the Convolutional Neural Network

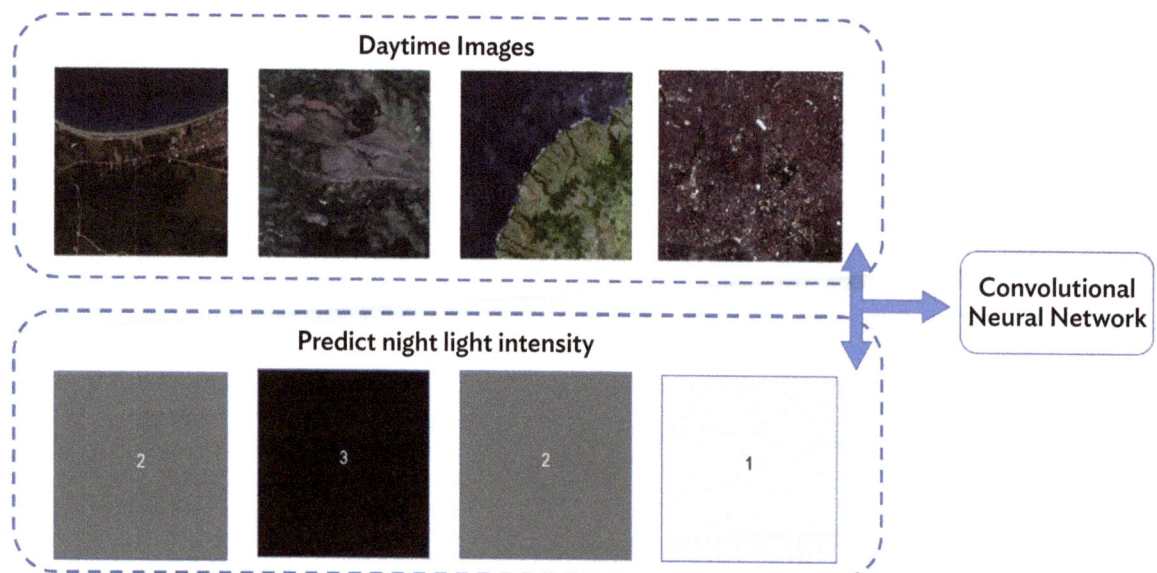

Note: These images were captured over several areas in the Philippines; from left to right: Claveria, Cagayan; Bagac, Bataan; Itbayat, Batanes; and Sta. Cruz, Manila.
Source: Sentinel 2 satellite.

Box 3.2: Convolutional Neural Network Implementation and Optimization

In the Asian Development Bank study on poverty mapping of the Philippines, the structure of the convolutional neural network (CNN) was enhanced by testing different combinations of network parameters. In conducting the CNN training, the number of epochs was optimized. The figure below illustrates the loss function of the algorithm, or how loosely the CNN predicted the intensity of night lights. The y-axis shows the loss for one epoch, while the x-axis shows the number of images the model had trained. The blue line shows the loss of the training set, while the orange line corresponds to the validation set.

Loss Function in Predicting the Intensity of Night Lights

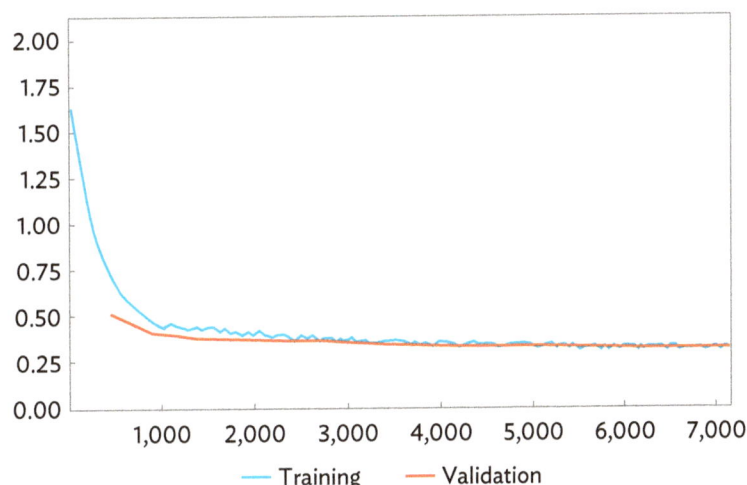

To minimize validation loss, the model was used with weights after the most successful sequence of epochs was used. Hence, during the training, an algorithm was applied that automatically monitored and saved the weights when an improvement was observed. When there was no improvement after training the epoch, weights were not saved, and instead the model was monitored for overfitting. A sign that overfitting has occurred is when the training loss starts to become significantly smaller than the validation loss. Overfitting also happens when validation loss stops decreasing.

Since a pretrained CNN model was used, there was a need to unfreeze the last two layers responsible for prediction, and replace them by training the model to predict the desired outcomes using the Philippine datasets. This is called transfer learning.

The study used a cyclical approach to learning rates in training the CNN model. This eliminated the need to experimentally find the best values and schedule for global learning rates. Instead of changing the learning rate for each layer, this method varies between a determined learning rate boundary. It achieves improved classification accuracy, without a need to fine-tune, and requiring fewer iterations.

Source: Calculations and graphics generated by the study team.

3.4 Extracting Features from the Convolutional Neural Network's Output Layer

After CNN implementation, the next step was the extraction of the satellite image features used in predicting night light intensity. As Figure 3.14 illustrates, these features are viewed numerically by the CNN as complex mathematical functions.

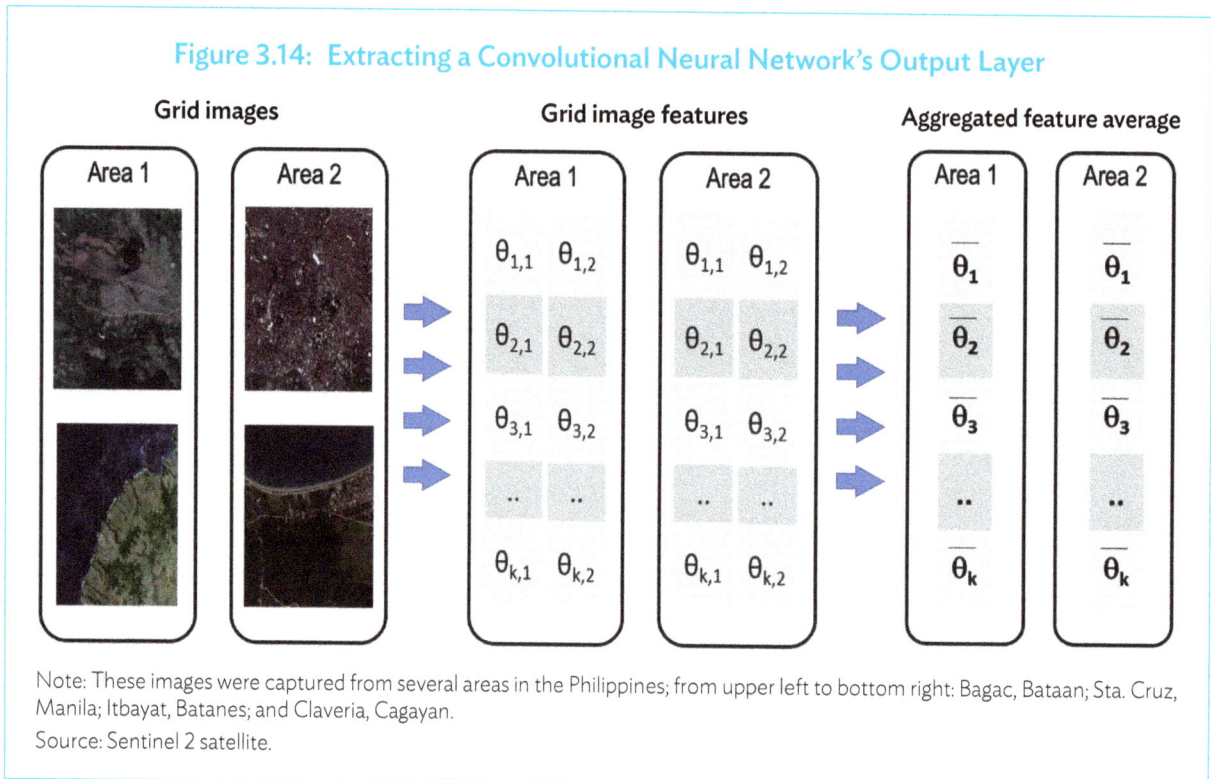

Figure 3.14: Extracting a Convolutional Neural Network's Output Layer

Note: These images were captured from several areas in the Philippines; from upper left to bottom right: Bagac, Bataan; Sta. Cruz, Manila; Itbayat, Batanes; and Claveria, Cagayan.
Source: Sentinel 2 satellite.

Because the main purpose of this study was to provide accurate poverty predictions, the average of the mathematical functions was taken and aggregated at the same geographic levels on which the government-published poverty estimates were compiled. Data were aggregated to municipality or city level for 2012 and 2015 and province level for 2018.

3.5 How Ridge Regression Models Translate Image Features into Poverty Predictions

The next step was to regress poverty rates on the aggregated data.

This study explored the advantage of using other estimation procedures, including the ordinary least squares (OLS) method, in selecting a regression technique. In general, OLS is able to find the best linear unbiased estimator, i.e., the parameters that best fit a given estimation sample. It uses every covariate and mixes them linearly. When the number of covariates becomes large, OLS will find parameters that fit the training data almost perfectly, but often fail to fit or predict additional data. With too many parameters, the underlying relationship between the covariates and the data might be found, but some of the noise that can lead to poor predictive performance also emerges.

Ridge regression, on the other hand, is a good proxy for OLS because it fixes OLS issues by penalizing large parameters to shrink unimportant ones toward zero. For those reasons, this study used the ridge regression technique.[24] The resulting coefficients of the ridge regression model were then applied to satellite image tiles with a 4-km by 4-km resolution to yield more granular poverty estimates.[25]

It is worth mentioning that, of approximately 1,600 cities and municipalities, 10% of the areas were randomly set aside to comprise the validation set, which was used solely for assessing the performance of the predictions. The CNN and the ridge regression training models employed supplemental training and test splits, distinct of each other. Specifically, tenfold cross validation was employed to adjust hyperparameters. These training sets were obtained after reserving the 10% validation set.

[24] Other modeling approaches like random forest estimation, support vector regression, and similar strategies can also be used.
[25] The level of granularity relies on the resolution of images employed and the extent of disaggregation of poverty data that are used as inputs. Hofer et al. (2020) give specific details.

4 Using Random Forest Estimation to Compile Grid-Level Estimates of Poverty Head Counts

An assessment of the poverty head count, or the number of individuals living below the poverty line at the grid level, was also covered in this study.

The initial step required calculating the number of individuals at the grid level and multiplying the number by the poverty rates predicted from the CNN ridge regression. This generated the poverty head count at the grid level.

Estimating grid-level population counts involved linking population census data with geographic information system-delineated administrative boundaries of Philippine cities and municipalities, which were the most granular administrative units with available information at the time of this study. The random forest estimation model included census data on log population density as the dependent variable and geospatial extracted data as the predictor variables. The list of potential predictor variables was identified from relevant research studies that established the high correlation of population distribution with land cover types and land cover data.

Information on land cover classes were sourced from GlobCover, a European Space Agency project that is designed to develop a service capable of delivering global composites and land cover maps. GlobCover produces high-quality and nonproprietary data with wide coverage. It also serves as the data source for several research works on estimating grid-level population size (Stevens et al. 2015). In addition to land cover classes, other geospatial variables included in the model were digital elevation data and the derived slope estimate sourced from HydroSHEDS data, net primary production derived from Moderate Resolution Imaging Spectroradiometer satellites, weather data from World Climate, night light intensity data from VIIRS, and other map features from Open Street Map.

The appendix to this report provides a summary of different variables employed to estimate population density at the 100 m x 100 m grid level. The majority of these variables have a constant resolution in degrees, and therefore the resolution in meters changes with the distance to the equator. The resolution presented in the appendix to this report indicates the approximate resolution near the equator.

The random forest approach was selected as the modeling framework, considering the range of benefits it offers. This approach can manage large sets of explanatory variables. It can manage both collinearity and nonlinearity issues, i.e., it deals with correlations between independent variables in the input data as well as the nonlinear relationship between the dependent variable and its independent variables. Random forest estimation also considers both bias and variance issues, because there is often a compromise between a model's bias and its variance in statistics and machine learning. In this case, neither bias nor variance should dominate. The random forest approach can limit both bias and variance in a reasonable way. The modeling framework can also cope with overfitting. Despite a very large set of training data, the model will not only reflect the dynamics of the training information, but will be able to make accurate predictions with new input data. Moreover, random forest can easily generate measures of variable importance, showing which independent variables are most important to finding accurate results. Lastly, with large sets of training data, the modeling framework can yield very precise estimates (ADB 2020).

The poverty mapping study in the Philippines applied a random forest of regression trees because the dependent variable (i.e., the number of people living in each 100 m by 100 m grid cell) is a continuous variable. The independent

Box 4.1: Introduction to Random Forest Estimation

The random forest approach is a model used to measure grid-level population density (Breiman 2001; Cutler, Cutler, and Stevens 2012). It is an ensemble learning method built on trees, where each tree is derived from a random subset of training data and a random subset of independent variables. A model can be made up of either classification trees or regression trees. The dependent variable identifies the type of trees to be employed in a specific random forest. The forest is generated from a set of classification trees if the dependent variable is discrete. The result of each tree in the forest is a classification of a dependent variable into one of a finite number of classes, and the class selected by most of the trees is employed as the result of the random forest. Meanwhile, the random forest includes a set of regression trees if the dependent variable is continuous. Each regression tree generates an estimate of the dependent variable, and the result of the random forest prediction consists of the average of all estimates generated by the individual trees. The figure below differentiates a random forest of classification trees and a random forest of regression trees.

Random Forest of Classification Trees versus Random Forest of Regression Trees

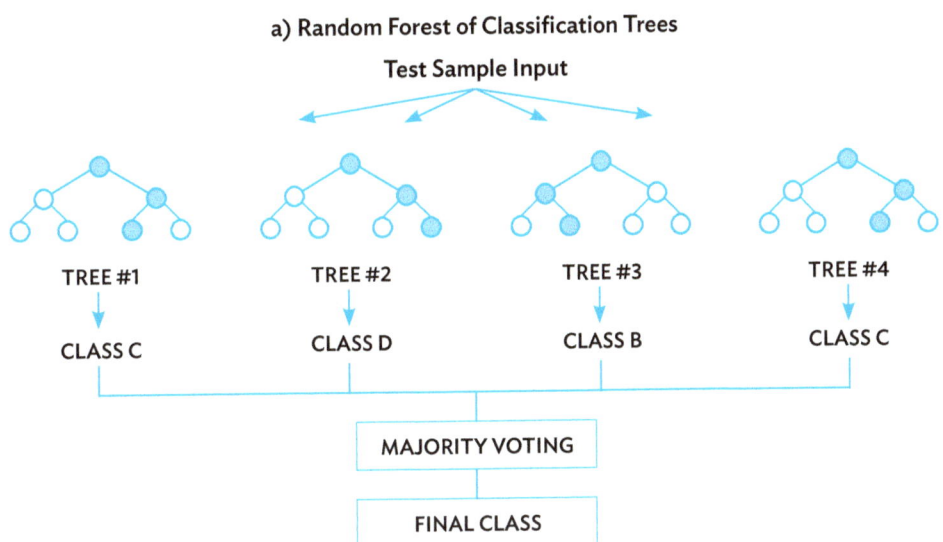

a) Random Forest of Classification Trees

Test Sample Input

TREE #1   TREE #2   TREE #3   TREE #4

CLASS C   CLASS D   CLASS B   CLASS C

MAJORITY VOTING

FINAL CLASS

Source: Medium website.

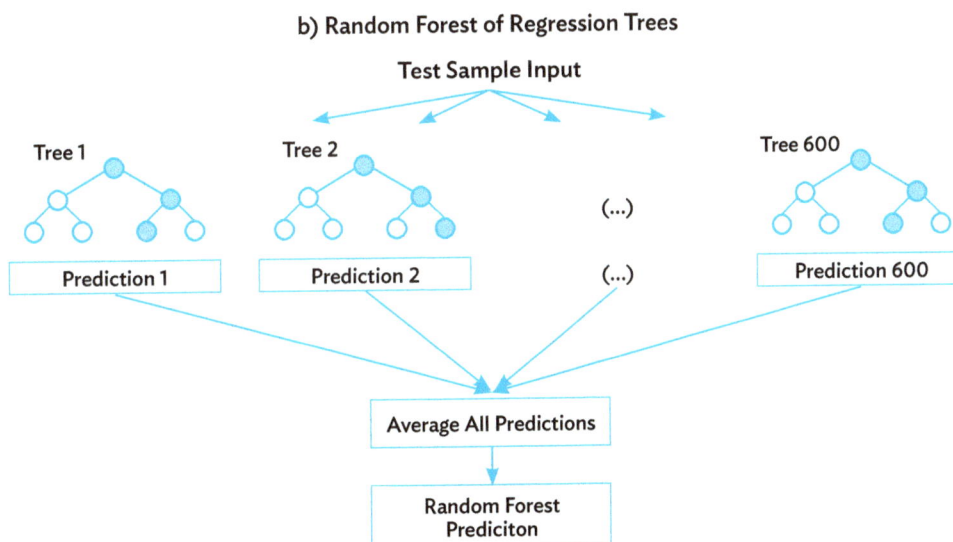

b) Random Forest of Regression Trees

Test Sample Input

Tree 1   Tree 2   (...)   Tree 600

Prediction 1   Prediction 2   (...)   Prediction 600

Average All Predictions

Random Forest Prediciton

Source: Towards Data Science website.

variables consist of satellite imagery data such as night lights, land cover classes, temperature, and precipitation. The vector of explanatory variables and the dependent variable are assumed to follow a joint distribution.

The objective of the study's random forest model was to identify a function for predicting gridded population. Under this model, a random forest is first generated from a set of regression trees. The regression trees are grown through the recursive binary splitting method, where each tree partitions the predictor space in a sequence of binary splits based on each independent variable. The first node, including the entire predictor space, is called the root node. The final nodes that are not split any further are called the terminal nodes. Considering a certain split point in the values of one of the independent variables, each nonterminal node is split into two descendant nodes. Values of the independent variable that are below this split point go to the left descendant node, while higher values go to the right one. To determine the exact split point to partition a node, every possible split in all independent variables considered in the tree is considered. In regression trees, the splitting criterion is based on the mean squared error of the predictions of the descendant nodes. After the selection of a split point, the node is divided into its two descendant nodes, which are again split in the same way. This procedure is repeated until either a predefined level of split or a predefined maximal tree size is obtained. Each of the trees can then be used to obtain an individual estimate of the gridded population. Finally, the unweighted average of the estimations of all trees provides the actual random forest prediction of gridded population.

5 Key Findings

In predicting poverty using geospatial data, the first step entails training a CNN model to predict night light intensity with the help of daytime images. Table 5.1 summarizes the prediction results. These are based on confusion matrices which are generated from the predictions of the CNN's output layer. These matrixes indicate the performance of the machine learning classification tasks.

The results indicate high overall prediction accuracy across the three reference years of 2012, 2015, and 2018. The CNN was able to accurately predict the night light intensity at low levels.[26] One possible rationale for this is that the features linked to low levels of night light intensity have similar structures that enable the algorithm to predict correctly.

The distribution of night light values also validates the good performance of the CNN. Because of limited and low night light values, the model can accurately predict low night light class areas where there are no or minimal observable human-made structures, resulting in higher prediction accuracy.

Table 5.1: Prediction Accuracy of Convolutional Neural Network

Data Set	2012	2015	2018
Validation set	94.15	93.50	92.91
Full data set	94.66	93.86	90.56

Source: Calculations generated by the study team.

As outlined, predicting night light intensity was just a transition phase to deriving satellite image features that are required to build a ridge regression model for predicting poverty. Some validation tasks were conducted to mathematically examine the predictive performance of the implemented method.

Calculating the root mean square errors (RMSEs) was the first validation task. Considering that the method adopted in this study generated poverty estimates at the grid level, the weighted average of grid-level poverty rates with gridded population estimates as weights (Chapter 4) were calculated to present all estimates at the city or municipality level. Table 5.2 indicates relatively low average prediction errors.

Table 5.2: Root Mean Square Error by Year

Year	Validation Set (%)	All (%)
2012	17	17
2015	17	15
2018	12	23

Source: Calculations generated by the study team.

---

[26] The overall prediction accuracy was calculated by dividing the number of correctly predicted images with the total number of images across rows.

Generating scatter plots, which provide a good visual picture of the overall fit and dispersion clusters, was another validation task. In Figure 5.1, each mark pertains to one city, municipality, or province. Blue marks correspond to the training set, while red marks correspond to the validation set. The x-axis provides the government-published poverty estimates, while the y-axis provides the poverty estimates based on machine learning. The marks clustering along the dashed straight line indicate good prediction performance.

Through the validation tasks, the study team examined the algorithm's performance in terms of how far the individually predicted poverty estimate deviated from its corresponding government-published estimate. Aside from numerical assessments, it was also essential to evaluate the spatial distribution of the estimates. Figure 5.2 shows the poverty maps where the poverty rates predicted via machine learning (illustrated at the 4 km by 4 km grid level) mirror the spatial distribution of the government-published poverty rates, i.e., the two sets of poverty estimates suggest similar patterns.

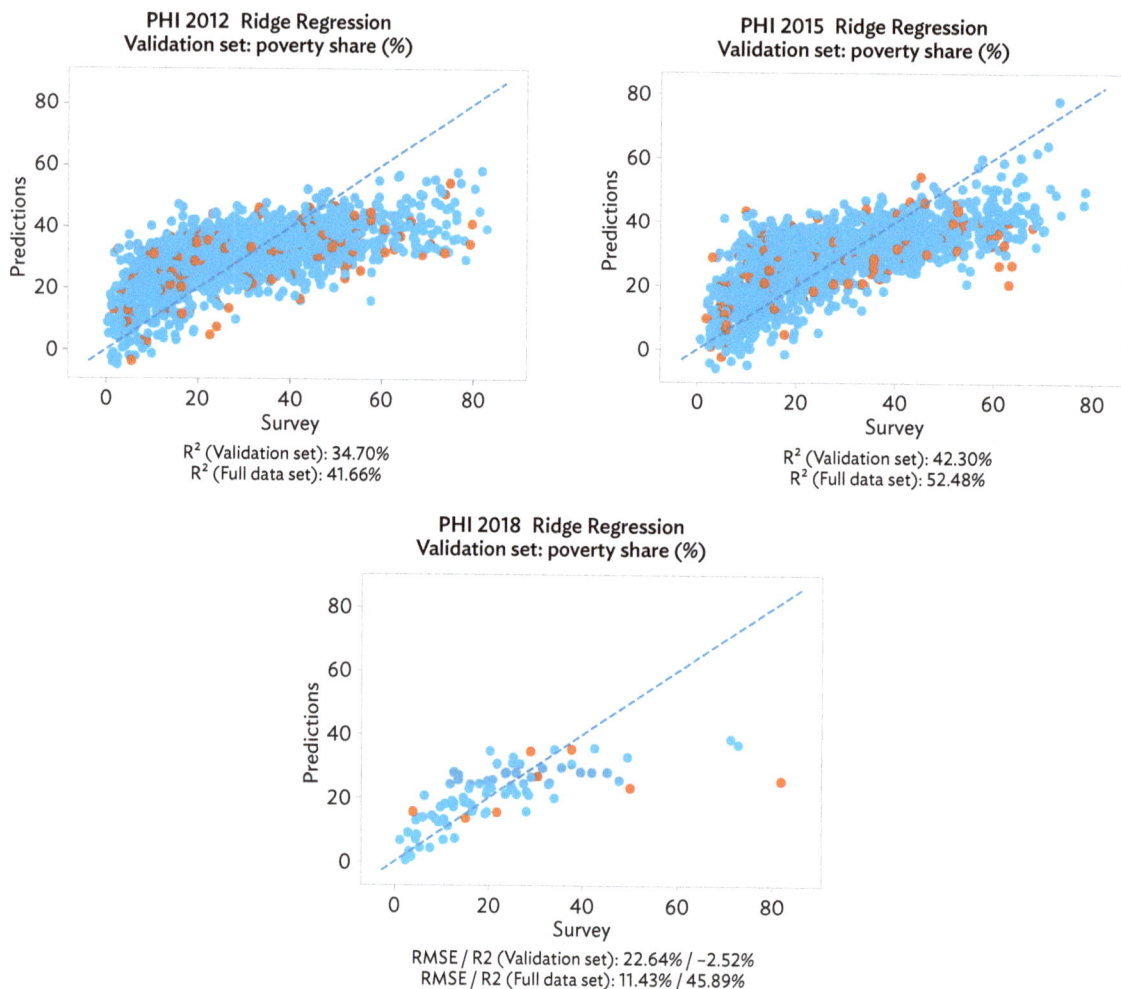

Figure 5.1: Scatter Plots of Published and Predicted Poverty Rates

PHI = Philippines, R^2 = r-squared.

Notes: The x-axis refers to the government-published poverty estimates for the year specified, while the y-axis refers to the predictions based on the machine learning model for the same year. The blue dots indicate the training set, while the red dots reflect the validation set.

Source: Calculations generated by the study team.

Figure 5.2: Maps of Published and Predicted Poverty Rates

PHI 2012, Published

Municipal
poverty rate:

- 0–20
- 20–40
- 40–60
- 60–80
- 80–100
- NA

PHI 2012, Predicted

Poverty rate per
4 km × 4 km

- 0–20
- 20–40
- 40–60
- 60–80
- 80–100
- NA

PHI 2015, Published

Municipal
poverty rate:

- 0–20
- 20–40
- 40–60
- 60–80
- 80–100
- NA

PHI 2015, Predicted

Poverty rate per
4 km × 4 km

- 0–20
- 20–40
- 40–60
- 60–80
- 80–100
- NA

continued on next page

Figure 5.2 *continued*

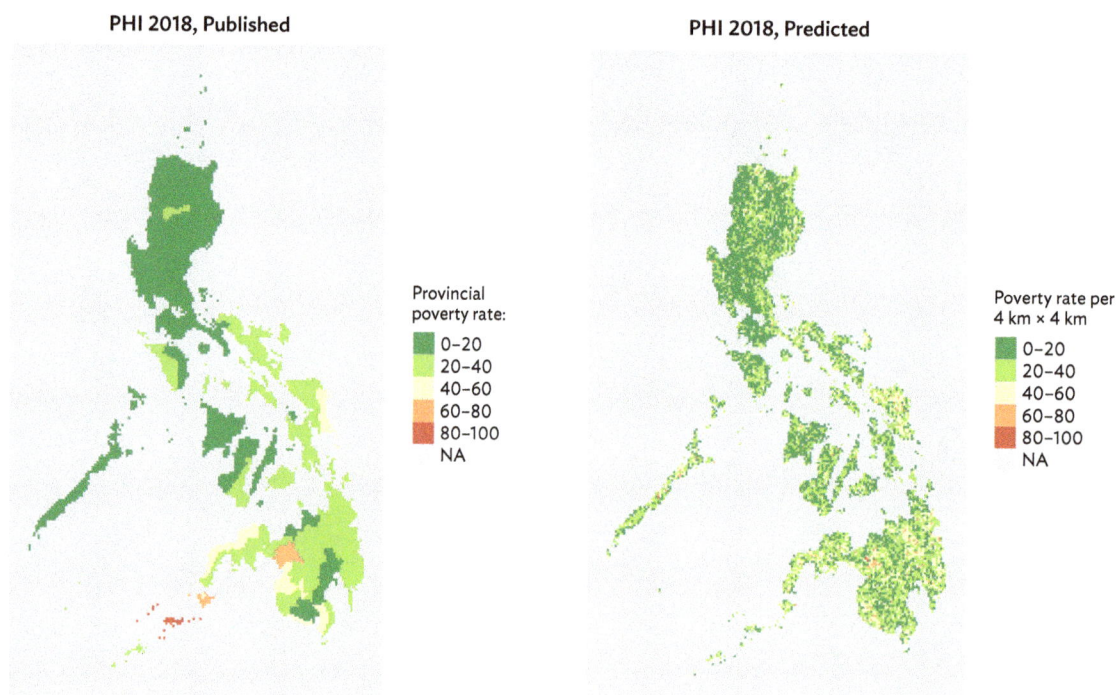

km = kilometer, NA = not applicable, PHI = Philippines.
Notes: The images present the municipal-, city- or provincial-level poverty rated published by the Philippine Statistics Authority in the first column, while the second column shows the machine learning estimates of poverty rates for every (approximately) 4-kilometer by 4-kilometer. These maps compare the poverty estimates arising from different methodologies. Researchers interested in understanding the factors that contribute to these poverty numbers should refer to socioeconomic reports.
Source: Calculations generated by the study team.

Some results, however, showed underestimation in the machine learning poverty estimates in areas with very high government-published poverty estimates. This is particularly true in some parts of northern and southern Philippines, where the government-published values were more than 60%, while the machine learning values were much lower.

5.1   Comparing Averaged Features and Averaged Outputs

There are two approaches to aggregating machine learning poverty rates at the same geographic level as the government-published poverty rates, i.e., city or municipality level for 2012 and 2015, and province level for 2018. The first approach is through ridge regression training, where averaged feature vectors are used and regressed on poverty rates. This approach can predict the government-published poverty rates in the sample for training and out of the sample for the validation set. Another approach uses image-level estimates. Trained ridge parameters are applied on the image-level features to derive image-level poverty rates. These poverty rates can be added to the geographic level of government-published estimates while controlling for population at the grid level.[27] In this study, the results of these approaches showed minimal differences in the RMSEs of averaged features and average outputs in all years covered.

---

[27] The study separately estimated grid-level population estimates following the approach of Stevens et al. (2015).

Table 5.3: Root Mean Square Error of Averaged Features and Averaged Outputs

Year	Averaged Features (%)	Averaged Outputs (%)
2012	13.30	15.00
2015	12.48	12.00
2018	22.64	23.00

Source: Calculations generated by the study team.

5.2   Validating Image-Level Estimates

Validating the image or grid-level estimates was a major constraint when there was no available ground truth image-level data to use for confirmation. Another concern was the aggregation of features and its effect on performance, considering there were two aggregation levels considered in this study: municipal or city level for 2012 and 2015 and the more aggregated provincial level for 2018. For 2018 estimates, more images per area were needed for aggregation.

To fully understand these issues, the study examined relatively small municipalities or cities possibly contained in a single daytime image. Thus, the aggregation step taken prior to the ridge regression and validation stages was no longer done. For 2015, there were 111 sole image areas added in the training set and 19 sole image areas in the validation set. Considering that the features no longer required aggregation or disaggregation, the ridge predictions were considered the final predictions of the grid-level poverty estimates. The ridge regression model was then rebuilt using this minimal set of areas.

The initial assumption was that the estimated model parameters could better measure the association between CNN-extracted features and poverty rates, because the aggregation or disaggregation step was already eliminated. Holding this assumption true, the model where single image areas were isolated was expected to have lower prediction errors (RMSEs) compared with the original model. However, results showed otherwise, i.e., relatively higher RMSEs were observed for the model based on single image areas only. It is deemed that these results were artificially driven by the fact that the estimation and training samples included very limited single image areas. Thus, the results are inconclusive in establishing whether the level of aggregation has a significant effect on the method's predictive performance, and may require further research.

5.3   Comparing Results with a Simpler Model Based on Night Lights

This study also conducted an exercise using a simpler model to assess whether this would perform better than complex models using daytime imagery and the deep-learning approach. The government-published poverty rates were regressed on the average night light intensity and an intercept using ordinary least squares. The results were used to estimate image-level poverty rates. Table 5.4 provides the summary of the resulting RMSEs.

Table 5.4: Root Mean Square Error for Poverty Rate (Validation)

Year	Artificial Intelligence-Based Model (%)	Simple Model Using Night Lights (%)
2012	13.30	17.86
2015	12.48	15.16
2018	22.64	17.12

Note: The model used city and municipal poverty rates for 2012 and 2015, and provincial poverty rates for 2018.
Source: Calculations generated by the study team.

In general, the model based on artificial intelligence produced smaller errors than the simple model, which only used night light intensity as the independent variable. The exception was the 2018 results, when the simple model showed better error estimates. These findings suggest that the machine learning approach is more sensitive to high-quality input data.

Table 5.5: Root Mean Square Error for Poverty Head Count (Validation)

Year	Artificial Intelligence-Based Model	Simple Model Using Night Lights
2012	24,460	15,938
2015	17,502	22,393
2018	125,445	193,283

Source: Calculations generated by the study team.

5.4   Comparing Uncalibrated Machine Learning Poverty Rates with Published Poverty Rates

This study investigated the robustness of the uncalibrated machine learning poverty estimates, when aggregated at the same geographic level as the government-published poverty rates. The results revealed that the machine learning method could correctly predict poverty for areas within the center of the distribution of the government-published poverty rates. However, the method tended to overestimate poverty in areas with low government-published poverty rates, while underestimating poverty in areas with high government-published poverty rates.

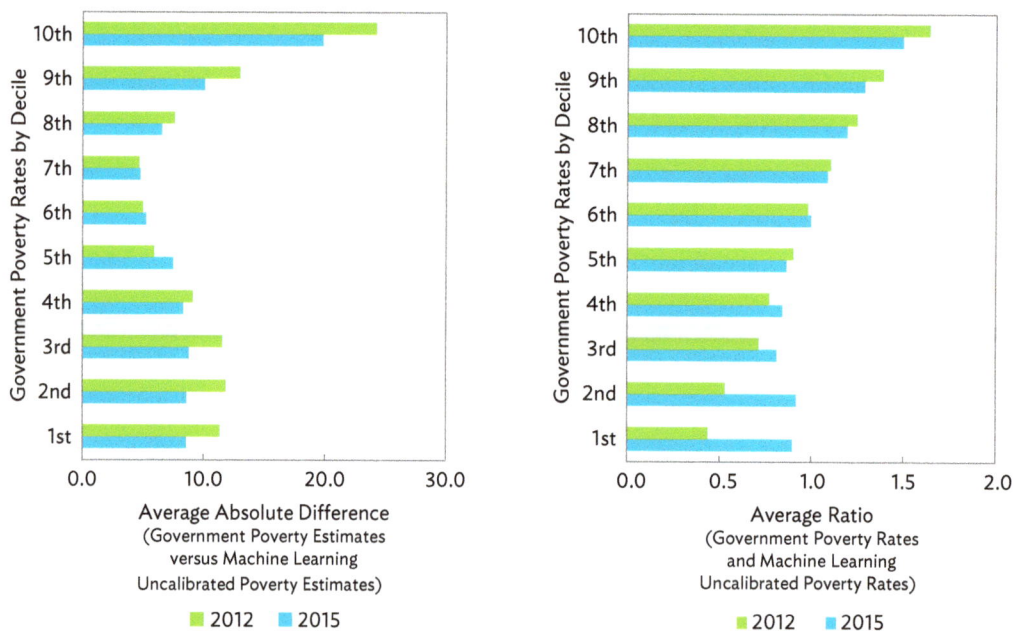

Figure 5.3: Average Absolute Difference and Average Ratio of Government Poverty Rates and Machine Learning Poverty Rates

Source: Calculations generated by the study team.

For 2012 and 2015, the published poverty rates (i.e., municipal and city poverty rates) categorized in decile groups and regions were compared with the corresponding machine learning poverty rates aggregated at the same geographical level, with the comparison based on the average absolute difference and average ratio of the two sets of estimates. The findings showed very minimal differences at the fifth, sixth, and seventh deciles, but large differences at the extreme ends of the distribution (Figure 5.3).

The study also tried to establish the validity of the poverty rates predicted via machine learning, with respect to the published measure of reliability of the government data. It examined if the predicted estimates lay within the published confidence intervals of the government estimates. The findings showed that more than 60% of municipalities and cities categorized in the sixth and seventh deciles had uncalibrated poverty rates falling within the 90% confidence interval of the published poverty rates. Meanwhile, less than 13% of municipalities and cities in the first and 10th deciles demonstrated the same pattern.

In five ARMM municipalities—Bacolod-Kalawi, Datu Paglas, Datu Saudi-Ampatuan, Shariff Aguak (Maganoy), and Wao—where published poverty rates exceeded 70% in 2012, the corresponding uncalibrated machine learning predictions were lower by more than 40 percentage points. Bacolod-Kalawi was the poorest municipality with an 84.8% poverty rate based on published data, but the predicted estimate was significantly lower at 37.5% using the uncalibrated machine learning approach. On the other hand, the uncalibrated machine learning poverty rate in

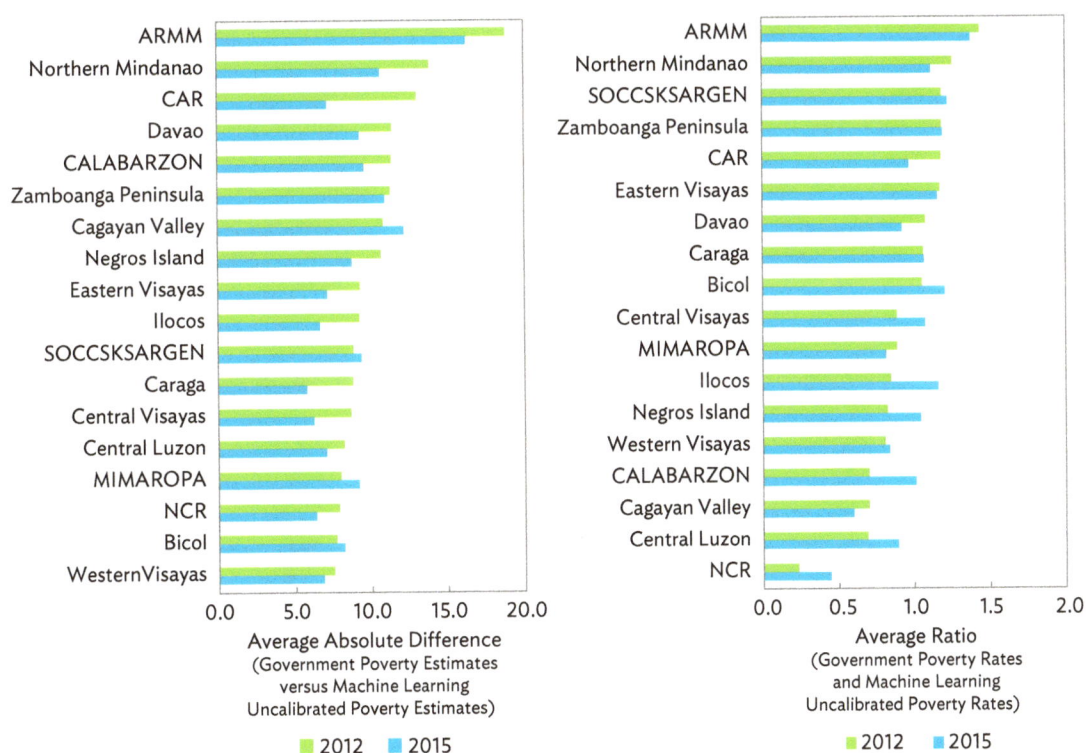

Figure 5.4: Average Absolute Difference and Average Ratio of Government Poverty Rates and Machine Learning Poverty Rates by Region

ARMM = Autonomous Region of Muslim Mindanao; CALABARZON = Cavite, Laguna, Batangas, Rizal, Quezon; CAR = Cordillera Administrative Region; MIMAROPA = Mindoro, Marinduque, Romblon, Palawan; NCR = National Capital Region; SOCCSKSARGEN = South Cotabato, Cotabato, Sultan Kudarat, Sarangani, General Santos City.

Source: Calculations generated by the study team.

Taguig City, located in the NCR, was 21.1% in 2012, which was significantly higher than the government-published poverty rate of 2.4%.

Figure 5.5 further illustrates the differences in the spatial distribution of the published and uncalibrated estimates of poverty rates at the municipal or city level.

Figure 5.5: Maps of Published and Uncalibrated Machine Learning Poverty Rates

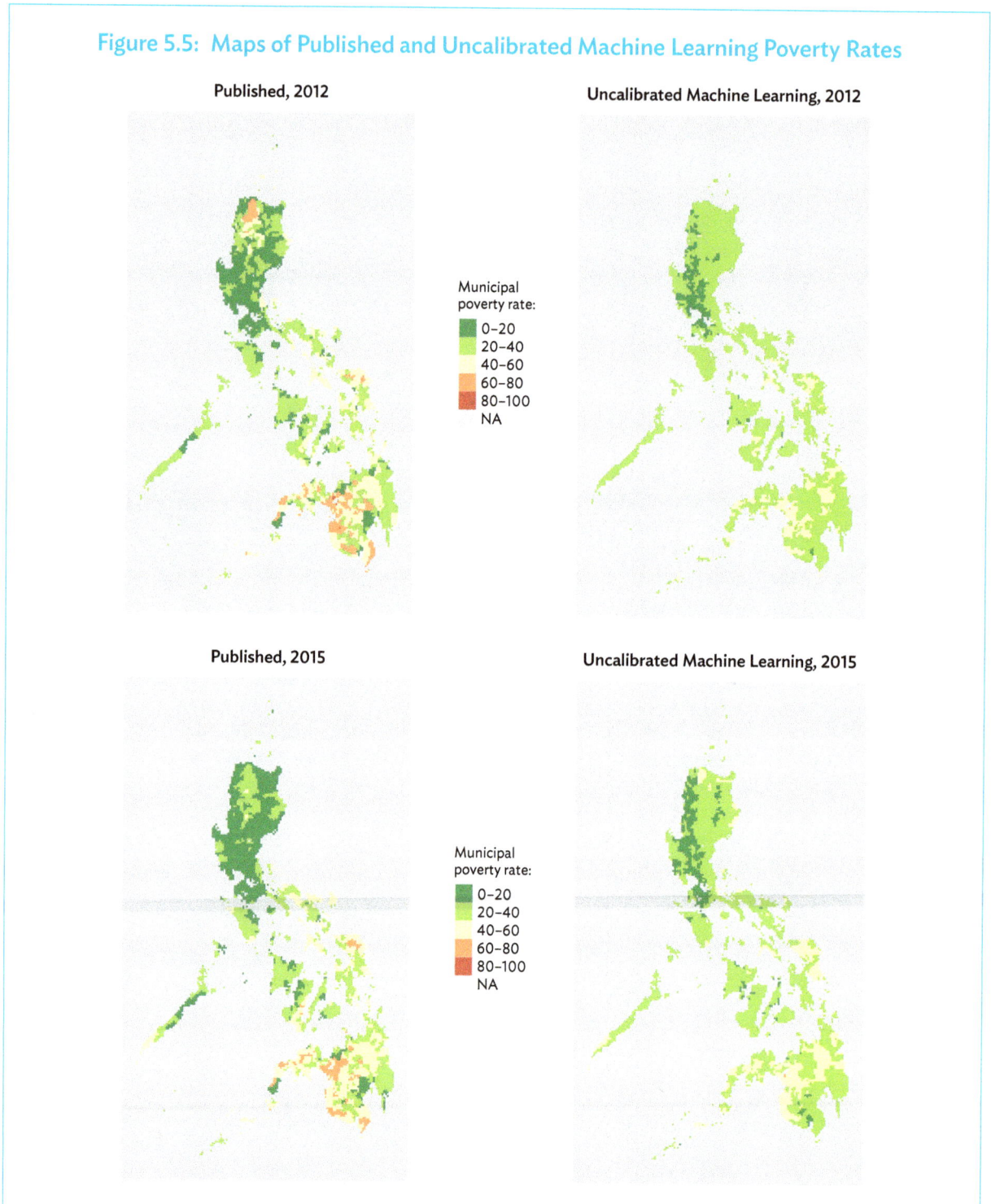

Published, 2012

Uncalibrated Machine Learning, 2012

Municipal poverty rate:
- 0–20
- 20–40
- 40–60
- 60–80
- 80–100
- NA

Published, 2015

Uncalibrated Machine Learning, 2015

Municipal poverty rate:
- 0–20
- 20–40
- 40–60
- 60–80
- 80–100
- NA

continued on next page

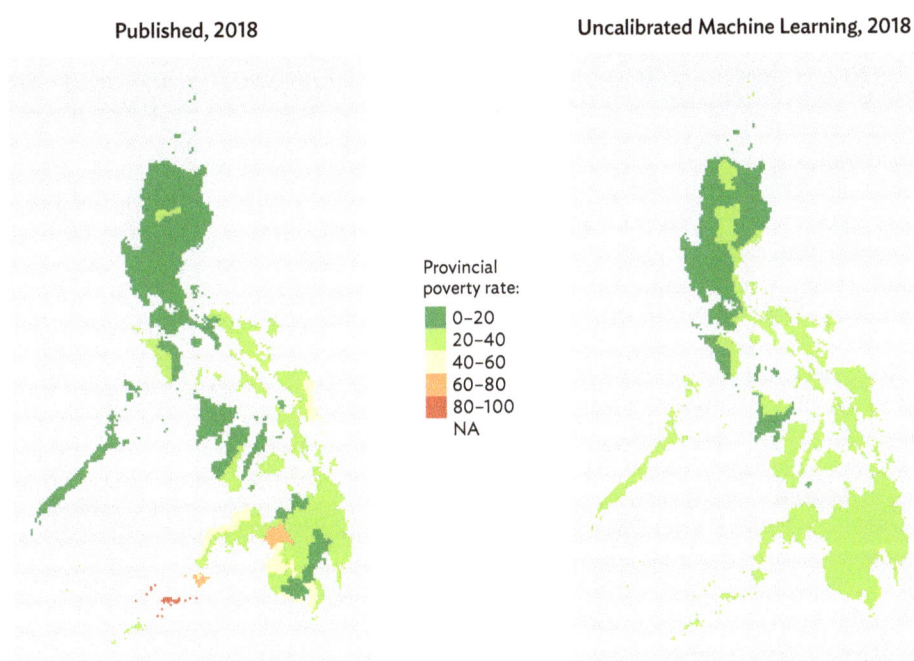

Figure 5.5 *continued*

Published, 2018

Uncalibrated Machine Learning, 2018

Provincial poverty rate:
- 0–20
- 20–40
- 40–60
- 60–80
- 80–100
- NA

Note: The first column presents images of municipal- or city-level poverty rates (for 2012 and 2015) and provincial poverty rates (for 2018) published by the Philippine Statistics Authority, while the second column shows uncalibrated machine learning estimates of poverty rates for every municipality or city (for 2012 and 2015) and for every province (for 2018).
Source: Calculations generated by the study team.

Meanwhile, the published poverty rates for 2018 (i.e., provincial poverty rates) grouped in quintiles and by regions were also compared with the corresponding machine learning poverty rates aggregated at the same geographical level, with the comparison based on the average absolute difference and average ratio of the two sets of estimates. The results indicated small differences at the fourth quintile and large differences at the first and fifth quintiles (Figure 5.6). Very large differences were noted between the published provincial poverty rates and the machine learning poverty rates in the ARMM (Figure 5.7).

5.5 Harmonizing Machine Learning Poverty Rates with Published Poverty Rates

Calibration methods can be employed to resolve possible overestimation or underestimation of poverty rates in some areas. Under the assumption that the government-published estimates provided a more accurate perspective of poverty at the municipal or city level (i.e., for 2012 and 2015) or province level (i.e., for 2018), the machine learning poverty rates could be calibrated to make the grid-level estimates, when aggregated at the particular geographic levels, consistent with the government-published data. Through calibration, one can also avoid creating confusion among poverty data users about choosing between the published and machine learning estimates, as the process creates internal consistency between the two datasets. Table 5.6 illustrates the poverty calibration method. It shows the published poverty data for a hypothetical municipality X and the corresponding machine learning estimates for the four grids within the municipality.

Figure 5.6: Average Absolute Difference and Average Ratio of Government Poverty Rates and Machine Learning Poverty Rates, 2018

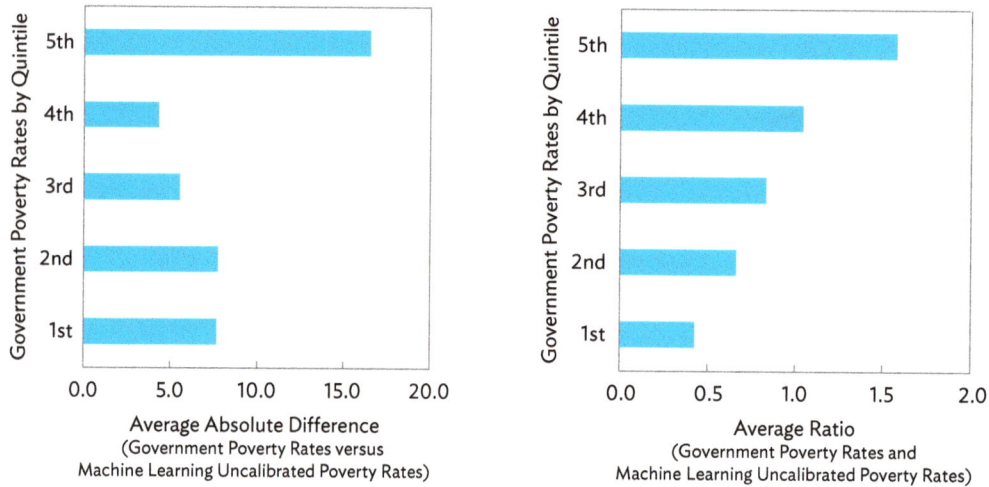

Source: Calculations generated by the study team.

Figure 5.7: Average Absolute Difference and Average Ratio of Government Poverty Rates and Machine Learning Poverty Rates by Region, 2018

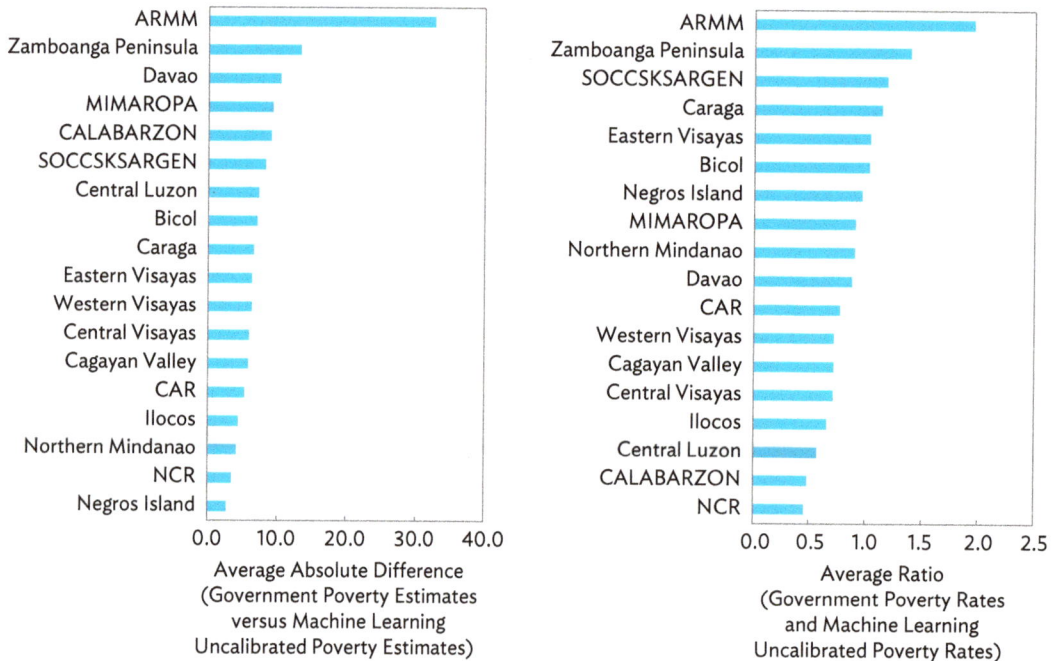

ARMM = Autonomous Region of Muslim Mindanao; CALABARZON = Cavite, Laguna, Batangas, Rizal, Quezon; CAR = Cordillera Administrative Region; MIMAROPA = Mindoro, Marinduque, Romblon, Palawan; NCR = National Capital Region; SOCCSKSARGEN = South Cotabato, Cotabato, Sultan Kudarat, Sarangani, General Santos City.

Source: Calculations generated by the study team.

Table 5.6: Sample Calculations for Calibrating Machine Learning Poverty Estimates with Published Poverty Estimates

Published data for Municipality X	Population Size (A)	Poverty Rate (B)	Poverty Head Count (A)*(B)		
	5,000	0.2	1000		
Machine learning data for grids within Municipality X	Population Size (C)	Poverty Rate (D)	Poverty Head Count (C)*(D)	Calibrated Poverty Rate [(A)*(B)/ sum(C*D)]*(C*D)/ (C)	Recalibrated Poverty Head Count [(A)*(B)/ sum(C*D)]*(C*D)
Grid # 1	1,250	0.17	213	0.21	263
Grid # 2	650	0.25	163	0.31	201
Grid # 3	2,500	0.12	300	0.15	372
Grid # 4	600	0.22	132	0.27	164

Source: Calculations generated by the study team.

There may be cases when the calibrated poverty rates do not significantly deviate from the original machine learning predictions (first row of Figure 5.8). There may also be cases when the two sets of poverty rates vary (second row of Figure 5.8). However, despite the differences in poverty levels, the rankings of the municipality or city poverty rates, based on the uncalibrated machine learning method, are expected to be preserved.

Rescaling will maintain the distributional structure of the grid-level poverty estimates and, at the same time, still reflect government-published estimates with higher aggregation levels. Implementing this calibration method may address potential confusion among conventional users of government statistics, who may be exploring nontraditional data sources. Figure 5.9 illustrates the spatial distribution of the calibrated grid-level estimates of poverty.

If there are issues with the accuracy of the government-published estimates, the uncalibrated machine learning estimates may be considered as inputs for validation. If there are insignificant differences between uncalibrated machine learning and government-published poverty estimates, then it is safe to assume that the two sets of estimates are reliable. On the other hand, substantial differences between the two sets may require additional investigation.

5.6 Comparing Calibrated Machine Learning Poverty Rates with Other Metrics of Poverty

The machine learning poverty rates at the 4 km by 4 km grid level were also aggregated at the barangay level—the lowest geographical unit of the Philippines—and compared with the Community-Based Monitoring System (CBMS) poverty estimates that are available for selected areas.[28]

---

[28] The 2012 CBMS poverty estimates cover five provinces (i.e., Benguet, Camiguin, Guimaras, Kalinga, and Surigao del Norte). The 2015 CBMS poverty estimates cover 11 provinces (i.e., Albay, Apayao, Aurora, Bohol, Camarines Norte, Camiguin, Ifugao, Marinduque, Occidental Mindoro, Romblon, and Tarlac) and 11 cities (Balanga City, Candon City, Escalante City, General Trias City, Marikina City, Paranaque City, Tabuk City, Tacurong City, Tanauan City, Tandag City, and Valenzuela City). The 2018 CBMS poverty estimates cover two provinces (Camarines Norte and Sarangani) and one city (Zamboanga City).

Figure 5.8: Calibration of Poverty Maps

Machine Learning Predictions   **Published**   **Calibrated**

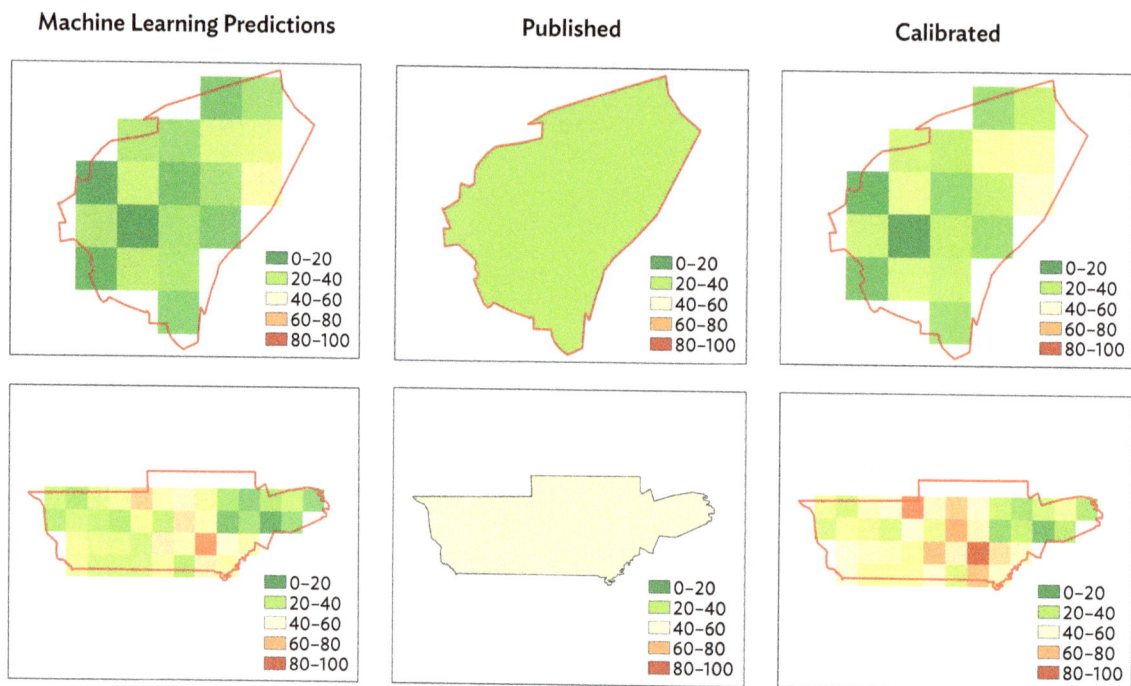

Source: Calculations generated by the study team, based on a hypothetical geographic location.

The CBMS is a local-level monitoring system that generates monetary and nonmonetary poverty indicators for selected provinces, municipalities, cities, and barangays in the Philippines. CBMS data collection is done by conducting household censuses using a household profile questionnaire and a barangay profile questionnaire. The household profile questionnaire consists of 12 pages, with one page dedicated to income questions. The data collected on total household income include aggregates of income (in cash and in kind) from entrepreneurial activities and/or sustenance activities, salaries and wages from employment, and other sources of income. The CBMS instrument generates the proportion of households with income below the official poverty line and the proportion of households with income below the official food poverty line (Reyes et al. 2019).[29]

Meanwhile, the poverty rates used in this study were based on official government estimates, which compare family income data collected via the Family Income and Expenditure Survey (FIES) with official food poverty lines and poverty lines.[30] Unlike the CBMS, which collects aggregate income data, the FIES gathers detailed family income data. Of the 80-page FIES questionnaire, 21 pages are devoted to collecting income data.

Correlation analysis was conducted to validate the calibrated machine learning poverty rates with the CBMS poverty estimates. This was done for select areas only, as CBMS does not compile poverty data for all areas. The correlation between the calibrated machine learning poverty rates and the CBMS poverty indicators was analyzed to establish the strength of the relationship between the variables of interest. For 2012 and 2015, the results suggest

[29] The total number of households with income below the poverty line over the total number of households, and the total number of households with income below the food poverty (subsistence) line over the total number of households, respectively (Reyes et al. 2019). The food and poverty lines are sourced from the PSA's official poverty statistics.

[30] Poverty incidence or the proportion of families or individuals with per capita income less than the per capita poverty threshold to the total number of families or individuals, and the subsistence incidence or the proportion of families or individuals with per capita income less than the per capita food threshold to the total number of families or individuals (PSA 2017).

Figure 5.9: Calibrated Machine Learning Poverty Rates

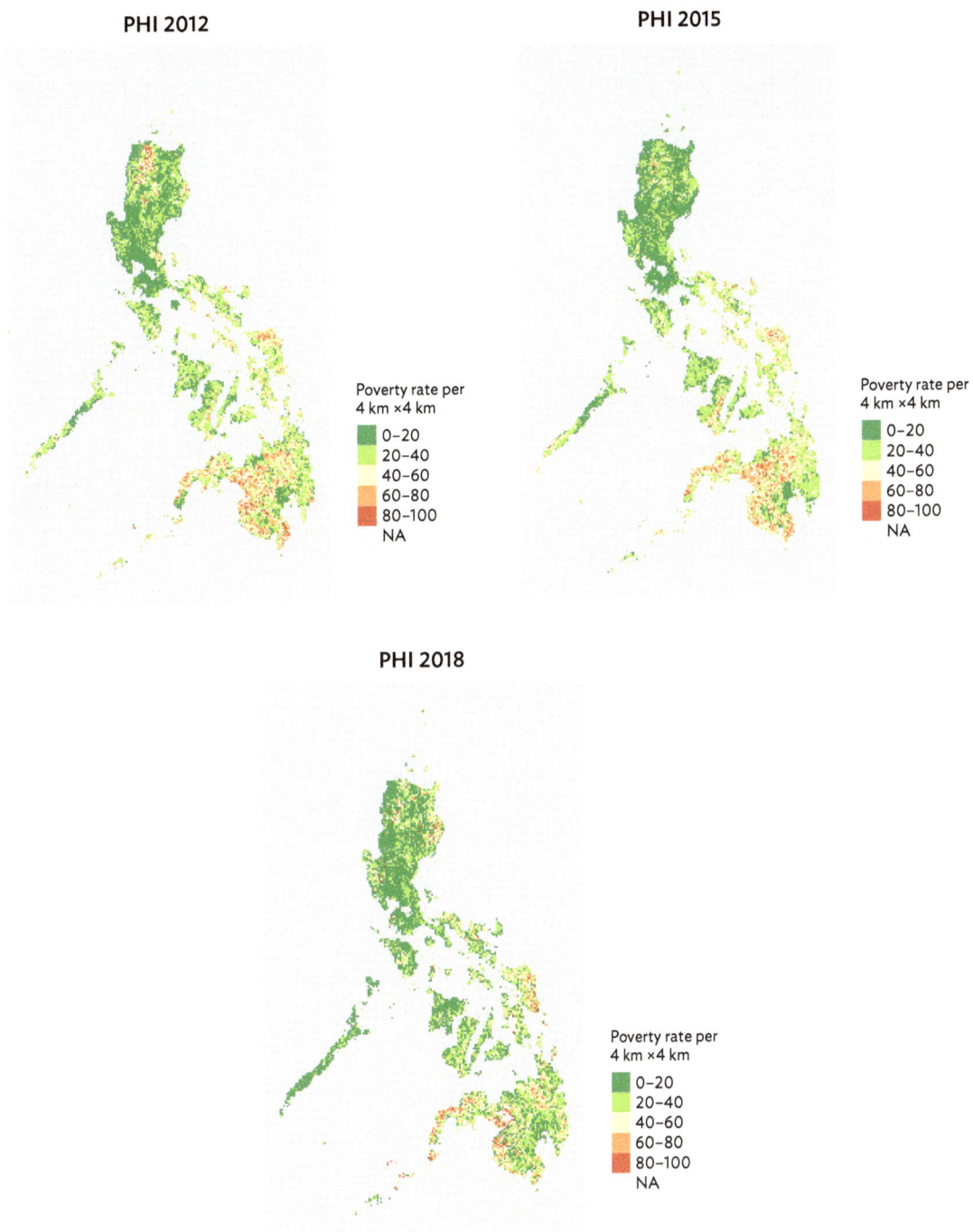

PHI 2012

PHI 2015

Poverty rate per
4 km ×4 km

0–20
20–40
40–60
60–80
80–100
NA

PHI 2018

Poverty rate per
4 km ×4 km

0–20
20–40
40–60
60–80
80–100
NA

km = kilometer, PHI – Philippines.
Note: The images present the calibrated machine learning estimates of poverty for every (approximately) 4-kilometer by
4-kilometer grid.
Source: Calculations generated by the study team.

weak to moderate correlation between the calibrated machine learning poverty rates and the CBMS poverty rates and food poverty rates. The study also validated the machine learning estimates with other correlates of poverty, with findings for 2015 indicating weak correlation between calibrated machine learning estimates and the following CBMS indicators: proportion of households without access to safe water supply, proportion of households without access to sanitary facilities, and proportion of children aged 12 to 15 years not attending high school. The difference in compiling poverty rates using the CBMS methodology and the government methodology could potentially explain these results.

5.7   Generating Grid-Level Estimates of Poverty Head Counts

Using the random forest approach, this study measured the poverty head count or the number of poor individuals at the grid level. Figure 5.10 shows the predicted poverty head count for every 4 km by 4 km grid level in the Philippines in 2012, 2015, and 2018. The results revealed a high concentration of predicted poverty head counts in many areas of Mindanao, where high poverty rates are recorded, as well as in some areas of the NCR, CALABARZON, Central Luzon, Central Visayas, and Western Visayas. Conversely, low concentrations of predicted poverty head counts were observed in many areas of Ilocos Region, Cagayan Valley, Cordillera Administrative Region, MIMAROPA Region, and parts of Eastern Visayas and Caraga Region.

Moving forward, the Technical Committee on Poverty Statistics which the Philippine Statistics Authority has reconstituted, is scheduled to review the methodology adopted in this study, as part of their initiative to review the current methodology of estimating official poverty in the country.

Figure 5.10: Random Forest Prediction of Poverty Head Count

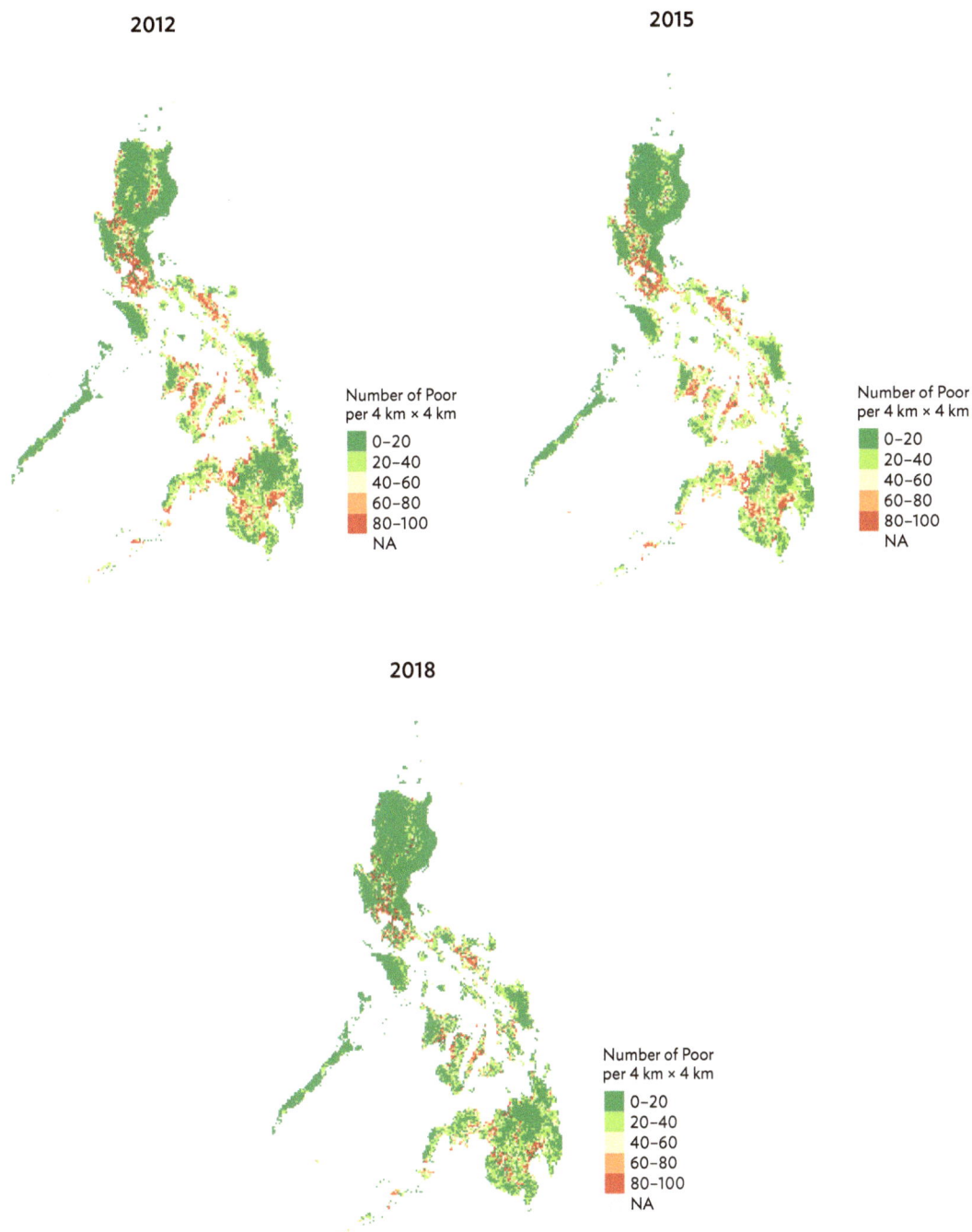

2012

2015

Number of Poor
per 4 km × 4 km

0–20
20–40
40–60
60–80
80–100
NA

Number of Poor
per 4 km × 4 km

0–20
20–40
40–60
60–80
80–100
NA

2018

Number of Poor
per 4 km × 4 km

0–20
20–40
40–60
60–80
80–100
NA

km = kilometer.

Note: The images present the random forest estimates of poverty head count for every (approximately) 4-kilometer by 4-kilometer grid in the Philippines.

Source: Calculations generated by the study team.

6 Summary and Conclusion

Advancements in digital technologies have resulted in a worldwide data revolution. At an unprecedented speed, volumes of data are being collected, managed, saved, retrieved, assessed, archived, unarchived, and reassessed. The landscape for providing statistical data to policymakers and program planners has also transformed, enabling many stakeholders to employ a continuing supply of data for decision-making. This challenges the framework that guides the conventional sources of official government data. The current framework depends considerably on censuses and sample surveys, which are not as capable or as cost-effective as digital data sources when it comes to generating disaggregated and timely evidence on which to base effective policies and implement targeted initiatives. There have also been instances when conventional data sources capitalized on administrative-based data that do not necessarily comply with the fundamental principles for collecting statistical data.

The need to adopt a new framework for gathering data for development cannot be overemphasized when the data requirements of the 2030 Agenda for Sustainable Development are taken into consideration. The data required for analyzing the progress of the 17 SDGs and their 169 corresponding targets call for huge resources from national governments, with their national statistical systems mandated to monitor 231 unique SDG indicators. The demand for granular data (i.e., by sex, age, income, residence) for these SDG indicators has further exerted pressure on collecting and compiling data for national statistical systems.

There are instances when funds allocated by the national government for statistical data collection and/or development are far from adequate. In these cases, NSOs must turn to development assistance provided by bilateral and multilateral organizations to fund their statistical development programs. This financial support, however, is generally insufficient and has hardly expanded in recent years (PARIS21 2017). It is even possible that funding for statistical development will contract in the wake of the global recession caused by government responses to the COVID-19 pandemic. Under these challenging circumstances, NSOs are required to be resourceful in addressing the data provisions of the SDGs, and several of them are assessing the merits of employing innovative data sources to improve development data generated from conventional sources.

Data from satellite imagery are not typically used for compiling official government statistics because they are naturally unstructured, distorted, and difficult to manipulate. However, the latest developments in machine learning methodologies, specifically in neural networks, have pushed the area of image analysis and paved the way for using satellite imagery to collect statistical data.

This poverty mapping study explored the potential use of satellite imagery in enhancing the geographical disaggregation of government-compiled poverty and population data in the Philippines, where the government releases poverty indicators at the municipal and/or city level every 3 years and population data at the municipal or city and barangay level every 5 years.

To improve the disaggregation of the country's existing poverty data, the study referred to the methodology employed by researchers at Stanford University—research that was featured in the journal *Science*. The methodology starts with training a CNN, an innovative machine learning algorithm often used in classifying images, to estimate night light data using daytime satellite images. Night light intensity sourced from satellite images is an excellent substitute for conventional welfare indicators and such images are accessible at geographically refined levels, which is essential in fulfilling the high volume of data needed to train a machine learning algorithm. During training of the CNN for this study, the algorithm managed to identify daytime image features associated with socioeconomic progress. The information derived from the images was then scaled up to match the geographic levels at which government-published poverty data were compiled.

The findings of this study using Philippine datasets are promising, despite employing nonproprietary images with resolutions that are not as refined as those in proprietary images. The poverty predictions were generally consistent with government-published poverty data, and the methodology produced more geographically disaggregated estimates of poverty.

Geographically refined poverty estimates are essential to effective policymaking and program planning to reduce poverty and inequality, with accurate statistical evidence needed at all levels of government. The COVID-19 pandemic also highlights the demand for high-quality, fine-grained data to respond to a range of health and economic issues. Such data may be made more accessible by looking at innovative ways to collect and assess it. ADB's Bayan Bayanihan is an example of an initiative that showcases how novel applications of big data and technological tools can inform the design of programs that benefit the poor. The poverty maps were used as inputs to identify target beneficiaries for such program that distributed essential food supplies to the poorest areas of Metro Manila during the onset of the lockdown to control the spread of the virus (Martinez and Mehta 2020).

NSOs are assessing different approaches to address the granular data demands of the development sector. The implementation of the small area estimation methodology—integrating survey, census, and auxiliary or administrative data—is one approach that a majority of NSOs have embraced. Additionally, some national governments are collaborating with local-level officials to improve the statistical capacities of staff in collecting localized data. The Government of the Philippines, for example, recently enacted a law authorizing the implementation of the Community-Based Monitoring System, which produces the timely and granular data needed for analysis of poverty and development indicators at the local level.

Employing satellite imagery as a proxy data source for predicting poverty is not intended to replace traditional data sources for poverty indicators. Rather, it aims to respond to some of the shortcomings of conventional poverty data availability. The data generated from more innovative approaches can also serve as reference points in confirming estimates generated via conventional methodologies, thereby ensuring the integrity of official government data.

NSOs should consider investing heavily in modern technology and capacity building to meet the development goals of the 21st century. Fine-tuning the methodology used in this study will entail access to higher-resolution satellite imagery and modern computing facilities. In most cases, any desire to combine big data into national statistical systems will also require collaboration with academic, private, and government institutions. Forming such alliances will guarantee a larger network for exchanging ideas, knowledge, and solutions on how to maximize innovative data sources in generating evidence for poverty reduction programs and a host of other urgent public policy challenges.

Description of Variables Used in the Estimation of Population Density

Type	Variable Name(s)	Description	Source
Census	y_data	Country-specific census and scale	National census, municipality level
Land Cover	globcover_cls11/ globcover_dst11	Post-flooding or irrigated croplands (or aquatic)	GlobCover, 300 m
Land Cover	globcover_cls14/ globcover_dst14	Rainfed croplands	GlobCover, 300 m
Land Cover	globcover_cls20/ globcover_dst20	Mosaic cropland (50–70%) / vegetation (grassland/shrubland/forest) (20–50%)	GlobCover, 300 m
Land Cover	globcover_cls30/ globcover_dst30	Mosaic vegetation (grassland/shrubland/ forest) (50–70%)/cropland (20–50%)	GlobCover, 300 m
Land Cover	globcover_cls40/ globcover_dst40	Closed to open (>15%) broadleaved evergreen or semi-deciduous forest (>5 m)	GlobCover, 300 m
Land Cover	globcover_cls50/ globcover_dst50	Closed (>40%) broadleaved deciduous forest (>5 m)	
Land Cover	globcover_cls60/ globcover_dst60	Open (15–40%) broadleaved deciduous forest/woodland (>5 m)	
Land Cover	globcover_cls70/ globcover_dst70	Closed (>40%) needleleaved evergreen forest (>5 m)	
Land Cover	globcover_cls100/ globcover_dst100	Closed to open (>15%) mixed broadleaved and needleleaved forest (>5 m)	
Land Cover	globcover_cls110/ globcover_dst110	Mosaic forest or shrubland (50–70%)/ grassland (20–50%)	GlobCover, 300 m
Land Cover	globcover_cls120/ globcover_dst120	Mosaic grassland (50–70%)/forest or shrubland (20–50%)	
Land Cover	globcover_cls130/ globcover_dst130	Closed to open (>15%) (broadleaved or needleleaved, evergreen or deciduous) shrubland (<5 m)	GlobCover, 300 m
Land Cover	globcover_cls140/ globcover_dst140	Closed to open (>15%) herbaceous vegetation (grassland, savannas or lichens/ mosses)	
Land Cover	globcover_cls150/ globcover_dst150	Sparse (<15%) vegetation	
Land Cover	globcover_cls160/ globcover_dst160	Closed to open (>15%) broadleaved forest regularly flooded (semi-permanently or temporarily)—Fresh or brackish water	GlobCover, 300 m
Land Cover	globcover_cls170/ globcover_dst170	Closed (>40%) broadleaved forest or shrubland permanently flooded—Saline or brackish water	GlobCover, 300 m
Land Cover	globcover_cls180/ globcover_dst180	Closed to open (>15%) vegetation (grassland, shrubland, woody vegetation) on regularly flooded or waterlogged soil— fresh, brackish or saline water	
Land Cover	globcover_cls190/ globcover_dst190	Artificial surfaces and associated areas (Urban areas >50%)	GlobCover, 300 m

continued on next page

Appendix Table *continued*

Type	Variable Name(s)	Description	Source
Land Cover	globcover_cls200/ globcover_dst200	Bare areas	
Land Cover	globcover_cls210/ globcover_dst210	Water bodies	GlobCover, 300 m
Land Cover	globcover_cls220/ globcover_dst220	Permanent snow and ice	GlobCover, 300 m
Protected Areas	protected_areas_100/ protected_areas_dist_100	Protected area	Protected Planet
Map Features	cities_100/ cities_dist_100	City	OpenStreetMap
Map Features	clinics_100/ clinics_dist_100	Clinic	OpenStreetMap
Map Features	hamlets_100/ hamlets_dist_100	Hamlet	OpenStreetMap
Map Features	hospitals_100/ hospitals_dist_100	Hospital	OpenStreetMap
Map Features	pharmacies_100/ pharmacies_dist_100	Pharmacy	OpenStreetMap
Map Features	railways_100/ railways_dist_100	Railway	OpenStreetMap
Map Features	rivers_100/ rivers_dist_100	River	OpenStreetMap
Map Features	schools_100/ schools_dist_100	School	OpenStreetMap
Map Features	suburbs_100/ suburbs_dist_100	Suburb	OpenStreetMap
Map Features	towns_100/ towns_dist_100	Town	OpenStreetMap
Map Features	villages_100/ villages_dist_100	Village	OpenStreetMap
Map Features	water_100/ water_dist_100	Water	OpenStreetMap
Elevation	hydro_ele_100	Elevation	HydroSHEDS, 100 m
Slope	hydro_slo_100	Slope	HydroSHEDS, 100 m
Net Primary Production	modis_100	Amount of carbon captured by plants	MODIS, 250 m
Precipitation	wc_prec_100	Monthly data on precipitation	WorldClim, 1 km
Temperature	wc_temp_100	Monthly data on temperature	WorldClim, 1 km
Nighttime Lights	night_lights_100	Lights at night	VIIRS, 500 m

< = less than, > = greater than, km = kilometer, m = meter, MODIS = Moderate Resolution Imaging Spectroradiometer, VIIRS = Visible Infrared Imaging Radiometer Suite.

Notes: The variable name with "cls" refers to a binary classification describing whether an area is covered by the given land cover class. The variable name with "dst" refers to the Euclidean distance to the next area covered by the given land cover class. The variable name without "dist" refers to a binary classification describing whether an area is covered by the given feature and the variable name with "dist" refers to the Euclidean distance to the next feature of this type.

References

Y. Akiyama. 2012. Analysis of Light Intensity Data by the DMSP-OLS Satellite Image Using Existing Spatial Data for Monitoring Human Activity in Japan. *Annals of the Photogrammetry, Remote Sensing and Spatial Information Sciences*. International Society for Photogrammetry and Remote Sensing. Hannover, Germany.

S. Amaral, G. Monteiro, G. Camara, and J. Qintanilha. 2006. DMSP/OLS Night-Time Light Imagery for Urban Population Estimates in the Brazilian Amazon. *International Journal of Remote Sensing*. 25. pp. 855–870.

Asian Development Bank (ADB). 2016. *Key Indicators for Asia and the Pacific 2016*. Manila.

—————. 2017. *Data for Development Technical Assistance Report*. Manila.

—————. 2018. *Asian Development Bank Member Fact Sheet Philippines*. Manila.

—————. 2019. *ADB Key Indicators Database 2019*. Manila.

—————. 2019. *Asian Development Outlook 2019 Update*. Manila.

—————. 2020. *Basic Statistics 2020*. Manila.

—————. 2020. Impact Evaluation of the Pantawid Pamilyang Pilipino Program. Manila.

—————. 2020. *Mapping Poverty through Data Integration and Artificial Intelligence: A Special Supplement of the Key Indicators for Asia and the Pacific*. Manila.

L. Breiman. 2001. Random Forests. *Machine Learning*. 45.1. pp. 5–32.

Brittanica. 2019. Philippines Plant and Animal Life. https://www.britannica.com/place/Philippines/Plant-and-animal-life.

C. Castelan, I. Weber, D. Jacques, and T. Monroe. 2019. Making a Better Poverty Map. World Bank Blogs. https://blogs.worldbank.org/opendata/making-better-poverty-map.

F. Chollet. 2017. Deep Learning with Python. Manning. ISBN: 9781617294433.

A. Cutler, D. R. Cutler, and J. Stevens. 2012. Random Forests. Ensemble Machine Learning. Springer. pp. 157–175.

D. Dai, L. Yu, and H. Wei. 2020. Parameters Sharing in Residual Neural Networks. *Neural Processing Letters*. 51. pp. 1,393–1,410. https://doi.org/10.1007/s11063-019-10143-4.

S. Das and R. Chambers. 2015. A Robust ELL Methodology for Poverty Mapping. 60th World Statistics Congress—International Statistical Institute 2015 Conference Paper.

Data 2x. 2017. Big Data and the Well-Being of Women and Girls Application of Social Scientific Frontier. https://data2x.org/wp-content/uploads/2019/05/Big-Data-and-the-Well-Being-of-Women-and-Girls_.pdf.

N. Eagle, M. Macy, and R. Claxton. 2010. Network Diversity and Economic Development. *Science*. 328 (5891). pp. 1029–1031.

C. Elbers, J.O. Lanjouw, and P. Lanjouw. 2003. Micro-Level Estimation of Poverty and Inequality. *Econometrica*. 71 (1). pp 355–364.

R. Engstrom, J. Hersch, and D.L. Newhouse. 2016. Poverty in HD: What Does High Resolution Satellite Imagery Reveal about Economic Welfare?

Exxact Corporation. 2019. TensorFlow 2.0: Dynamic, Readable, and Highly Extended (Blog Post). https://blog.exxactcorp.com/tensorflow-2-0-dynamic-readable-and-highly-extended/.

T. Ghosh, R. Powell, C. Elvidge, K. Baugh, P. Sutton and S. Anderson. 2010. Shedding Light on the Global Distribution of Economic Activity. *The Open Geography Journal*. 3. pp. 147–160.

I. Goodfellow, Y. Bengio, and A. Courville. 2016. *Deep Learning*. MIT Press. London.

Government of the Philippines. 2019. About the Philippines. https://www.gov.ph/about-the-philippines.

Government of the Philippines, Department of Social Welfare and Development (DSWD). 2018. Implementing Guidelines for the Unconditional Cash Transfer Program. https://www.dswd.gov.ph/issuances/MCs/MC_2018-003.pdf.

———. 2018. Philippines Conditional Cash Transfer Program Impact Evaluation 2012. https://pantawid.dswd.gov.ph/wp-content/uploads/2018/09/IE-Wave-1-Executive-Summary-1.pdf.

———. 2019. Kapit-Bisig Laban sa Kahirapan-Comprehensive and Integrated Delivery of Social Services. https://ncddp.dswd.gov.ph/site/page/1.

———. 2019. Omnibus Guidelines in the Implementation of the Social Pension for Indigent Senior Citizens. https://www.dswd.gov.ph/issuances/MCs/MC_2019-004.pdf.

Government of the Philippines, National Economic and Development Authority (NEDA). 2017. Philippine Development Plan 2017–2022. http://www.neda.gov.ph/philippine-development-plan-2017-2022/.

———. 2019. Statement on the Poverty Statistics for the First Half of 2018. http://www.neda.gov.ph/statement-on-the-poverty-statistics-for-the-first-half-of-2018/.

A. Hannun. 2017. PyTorch or TensorFlow? Github. https://awni.github.io/pytorch-tensorflow/.

M. Hofer, T. Sako, A. Martinez, J. Bulan, M. Addawe, R. Durante, and M. Martillan. 2020. Applying Artificial Intelligence on Satellite Imagery to Compile Granular Poverty Statistics. https://www.adb.org/publications/artificial-intelligence-satellite-imagery-poverty-statistics.

D. Hutchins, M. Herreshoff, and M. Looks. 2020. TensorFlow Fold. Github. https://github.com/tensorflow/fold.

N. Jean, M. Burke, M. Xie, M. Davis, D. Lobell, and S. Ermon. 2016. Combining Satellite Imagery and Machine Learning to Predict Poverty. *Science*. 353 (6301). pp. 790–794.

A. Krizhevsky, I. Sutskever, and G. Hinton. 2012. ImageNet Classification with Deep Convolutional Neural Networks. http://www.cs.toronto.edu/~hinton/absps/imagenet.pdf.

V. Kurama. 2020. PyTorch vs. TensorFlow: Which Framework Is Best for Your Deep Learning Project? *Built In*. https://builtin.com/data-science/pytorch-vs-tensorflow.

C. P. Lo. 2001. Modelling the Population of China Using DMSP Operational Linescan System Nighttime Data. *Photogrammetric Engineering & Remote Sensing*. 67. pp. 1037–1047.

S. Marchetti, C. Giusti, M. Pratesi, N. Salvati, F. Giannotti, D. Pedreschi, S. Rinzivillo, L. Pappalardo, and L. Gabrielli. 2015. Small Area Model-Based Estimators Using Big Data Sources. *Journal of Official Statistics*. 31 (2). pp. 263–281.

A. Martinez and A. Mehta. 2020. How Satellite Data Helped Get Food to the Hungry During COVID-19. https://development.asia/explainer/how-satellite-data-helped-get-food-hungry-during-covid-19.

Medium. 2018. Applying Random Forest (Classification): Machine Learning Algorithm from Scratch with Real Datasets. https://medium.com/@ar.ingenious/applying-random-forest-classification-machine-learning-algorithm-from-scratch-with-real-24ff198a1c57.

Millennium Development Goals Monitor. 2016. MDG Progress Report of Asia and the Pacific in 2015. https://www.mdgmonitor.org/mdg-progress-report-asia-the-pacific-2015/.

S. Pandey, T. Agarwal, and N. Krishnan. 2018. Multi-Task Deep Learning for Predicting Poverty from Satellite Images. Thirty Second AAAI Conference on Artificial Intelligence.

Partnership in Statistics for Development in the 21st Century. 2017. *Partner Report on Support to Statistics Press 2017*. Paris.

L. Perez and J. Wang. 2017. The Effectiveness of Data Augmentation in Image Classification using Deep Learning. arXiv preprint arXiv:1712.04621.

Philippine Institute for Development Studies. 2020. Pantawid Pamilyang Pilipino Program Third Wave Impact Evaluation (IE Wave 3) Regression Discontinuity Report. Manila.

Philippine Statistics Authority (PSA). 2003. Notes on the Official Poverty Statistics in the Philippines. Manila.

————. 2005. Estimation of Local Poverty in the Philippines. Manila.

————. 2007. Glossary of Terms. Manila.

————. 2013. 2006 and 2009 Municipal and City Level Poverty Estimates. Manila.

————. 2016. Philippine Population Density (Based on the 2015 Census of Population). Manila.

————. 2016. PSA Conducts the Country Workshop on Access to New Data Sources for Official Statistics: Business Models for Big Data. Manila.

————. 2016. PSA Memorandum Order No. 7 Series of 2016 Creating the Task Force on Big Data for Official Statistics. Manila.

————. 2016. 2012 Municipal and City Level Poverty Estimates. Manila.

————. 2017. PSA Resolution No.1, Series of 2017 – 171 Annex. Manila.

————. 2017. Technical Notes on the Estimation of Poverty Statistics Among the Basic Sectors. Manila.

————. 2018. Philippine Statistical Development Program 2018–2023. Manila.

————. 2019. Urban Population in the Philippines (Results of the 2015 Census of Population). Manila.

————. 2019. 2015 Municipal and City Level Poverty Estimates. Manila.

————. 2020. Farmers, Fisherfolks, Individuals Residing in Rural Areas and Children Posted the Highest Poverty Incidences Among the Basic Sectors in 2018. Manila.

————. Sustainable Development Goals. https://psa.gov.ph/sdg/Philippines/introduction.

S. Piagessi, L. Gauvin, M. Tizzoni, N. Adler, S. Verhulst, A. Young, R. Price, L. Ferres, C. Cattuto, and A. Panisson. 2019. Predicting City Poverty Using Satellite Imagery. *The IEEE Conference on Computer Vision and Pattern Recognition (CVPR) Workshops*. pp. 90–96.

R. Pizatella-Haswell. 2018. Fighting Poverty with Big Data: A Conversation with Joshua Blumenstock. Blum Center for Developing Economies. https://blumcenter.berkeley.edu/uncategorized/fighting-poverty-with-big-data-a-conversation-with-joshua-blumenstock/.

C. Reyes, A. Mandap, J. Quilitis, J. Nabiong, N. Kuan, C. Predo, K. Madrelino, M. Nicolas, and A. Gregorio. 2019. The Many Faces of Poverty Volume 10. De La Salle University Publishing House. Manila.

F. Stevens, A. Gaughan, C. Linard, and A. Tatem. 2015. Disaggregating Census Data for Population Mapping Using Random Forests with Remotely-Sensed and Ancillary Data. PLoS One. https://journals.plos.org/plosone/article?id=10.1371/journal.pone.0107042.

P. Sutton. 1997. Modelling Population Density with Night-Time Satellite Imagery and GIS. *Computers, Environment and Urban Systems*. 21 (3/4). pp. 227–244.

Towards Data Science. 2019. Random Forest Regression: Along with Its Implementation in Python. https://towardsdatascience.com/random-forest-and-its-implementation-71824ced454f.

United Nations. 1995. *Report of the World Summit for Social Development*. Copenhagen.

————. 2005. *Handbook on Poverty Statistics: Concepts, Methods and Policy Use*. United Nations Statistics Division. Copenhagen.

United Nations, Department of Economics and Social Affairs, Statistics Division. 2017. Sustainable Development Goals Cape Town Global Action Plan for Sustainable Development Data. Copenhagen.

————. 2019. Sustainable Development Goals Knowledge Platform Philippines. Copenhagen.

United Nations Global Pulse. 2018. Measuring Poverty with Machine Roof Counting. https://www.unglobalpulse.org/projects/measuring-poverty-machine-roof-counting.

United Nations Task Team on Satellite Imagery and Geo-spatial Data. 2017. Earth Observations for Official Statistics: Satellite Imagery and Geospatial Data Task Team report. https://unstats.un.org/bigdata/task-teams/earth-observation/UNGWG_Satellite_Task_Team_Report_WhiteCover.pdf.

World Bank. 2019. The World Bank in the Philippines. https://www.worldbank.org/en/country/philippines/overview#1.

R. Yamashita, M. Nishio, R. Do, and K. Togashi. 2018. Convolutional Neural Networks: An Overview and Application in Radiology. *Insights into Imaging*. 9. pp. 611–629. https://doi.org/10.1007/s13244-018-0639-9.

Y. Zhou, T. Ma, C. Zhou, and T. Xu. 2015. Nighttime Light Derived Assessment of Regional Inequality of Socioeconomic Development in China. *Remote Sensing*. 7. pp. 1242–1262.